FOREWORD BY
BILL LEWIS

THE
iNNOVATOR

LIFE Leadership Essentials Series

OBSTACLÉS
PRESS

First Edition, August 2015
10 9 8 7 6 5 4 3 2 1

Published by:

Obstaclés Press
200 Commonwealth Court
Cary, NC 27511

lifeleadership.com

ISBN 9780996461269

Cover design and layout by Norm Williams, nwa-inc.com

Printed in the United States of America

CONTENTS

PART THREE: THE PRACTICE

FOREWORD
by Bill Lewis

Instead of being called *The Innovator*, this book could easily be titled *How to Run a Successful Company* or *How to Succeed at Anything*. The content is truly amazing and will help make innovation your ally. As one of my mentors, Orrin Woodward, often says, "We overestimate what we can do in one year and drastically underestimate what we can do in ten years." That's because we don't understand the *compounding power of innovation*.

Most of us have heard the maxim "Innovate or die." And most of us know there is truth in that statement. But unfortunately, many of us just gloss over that idea without making innovation a priority. We talk about how important innovation is, but the skills and principles for innovating are rarely taught. There are few books or other resources that actually provide a *blueprint* for innovation. This book does. It not only teaches you how to create an innovative environment; it also reveals what to avoid, how to innovate in both large and small companies, the crucial financial thought process you need to employ, and how to leverage innovative ideas for optimum results.

As Bill Gates has said, in our society where things are changing at the speed of thought, companies must innovate quickly and make innovation a normal part of their culture. Properly implementing ideas for new products and services as well as ones that make current products and services better is critical for ongoing success.

I come from an engineering Tier 1 automotive supplier background, and I saw first-hand how the company I worked for used some of the principles *The Innovator* teaches. But what I saw even more often was how they violated the majority of them. They did not consistently apply and excel in all six stages of effective innovation.

And whether we are aiming to innovate at an organizational level or a societal level, it's always a good idea to start at the individual level. The number one thing I see people fail at is innovating themselves. Whether it's from fear of changing or simply not knowing the process, lack of growth and change puts all of us at a disadvantage. We can blame the rest of the world, or we can grow, innovate, change, and then start moving forward.

I tell organizations all the time that there is a shortcut to success, but it's only a shortcut because so few people use it. It is learning from others who have already succeeded at what you want to achieve. And this book enables you to do just that. The world we live in is constantly changing and evolving, and this book will not only make you feel comfortable with change; it will help you harness the power of effective innovation and excel as the Innovator.

IT'S TIME!

Yesterday is gone. Tomorrow has not yet come.
We have only today. Let us begin.
—Mother Teresa

The truth is it's time.

It's time right *now*.

Time for what? Time to innovate. How do we know? Because it's always time to innovate. Those who don't innovate fall behind. They lose their edge. They stop progressing. They plateau, at best. At worst…things get really bad.

No matter how successful you've been up to this point, if you stop innovating, you'll see your gains diminish and your achievements fade with time. Success is a process, not a destination. And an essential part of the process is consistent innovation.

Leaders innovate. Period. Unless they do, they aren't actually *leading*.

In fact, nobody becomes a real leader without effective innovation, and every top leader knows that innovation is vital to continued

> **Leaders innovate. Period. Unless they do, they aren't actually *leading*.**

movement. The old proverb "Innovate or die" is still true, at least in a leadership and business sense.

Some people want to be leaders, and in fact work hard to do almost everything that is necessary to fully reach their potential, but then fall just short of their goals because they can't seem to become truly innovative. Some are innovative for a time but then plateau and focus mostly on other things, forgetting that innovation must be part of every successful week, month, and year.

On the other extreme, some would-be leaders get so caught up in innovation that they never get past the first few steps of the process, instead quitting when things are just heating up for success. These people seldom consider themselves quitters because they are always working hard. Sadly, they jump from project to project, always stuck in the first two stages of innovation and never making the leap to the vital later stages.

Innovation must be a continued, day-in-day-out process. Wherever your company, business, community, or leadership is right now, it could soon stand to benefit from some real and powerful innovation.

This means prospective leaders must avoid the regular human tendency to fall into one or both of these lackluster innovative extremes.

Orrin Woodward teaches that people tend to overestimate what they can accomplish in one year and underestimate what they can achieve in ten. When it comes to innovation, this is extremely relevant! Often we believe too much in the power of one small innovation and call it a good change before the desired impact is truly put into effect. In doing so, some are led to believe that everything has been accomplished, yet what was really needed was a series of *ten* powerful and successive innovations.

> **Those who seek to be truly successful innovators must learn to make each new year — and each *innovation* — full of its own new experiences, lessons, and innovative *actions*.**

Of course, Woodward reminds us, thirty years of experience is not the same as one year of experience repeated thirty times in a row. This difference is real, and those who seek to be truly successful innovators must learn to make each new year — and each *innovation* — full of its own new experiences, lessons, and innovative *actions*.

One big innovation followed by stagnancy is clearly not enough to achieve continued movement and growth. However, "innovating" in a way that doesn't build on past innovations—even if it's applied in seemingly different ways, in different groups or settings, or in different career fields—isn't really innovating. It's just needlessly repeating what's already been done rather than continuing the process to the point of real and actual progression.

In short, truly innovative leaders are those who boldly and creatively take step after step after step in the right direction—neither stopping after a single step nor stepping with the same foot over and over in a way that only takes them in circles.

> **Truly innovative leaders are those who boldly and creatively take step after step after step in the right direction.**

Yet many people who seek to achieve real leadership seem to find themselves instead on the path of one of these processes of merely *attempting* innovation—failing to follow through with meaningful innovation or even get started!

The Zeitgeist

Indeed, successful and consistent innovation is elusive for *most* people. The few who figure it out and then apply it steadily, over and over, naturally achieve top leadership—in whatever they choose as their field of influence. Others simply don't make it to this point.

> **Without innovation, leadership shrinks, successes remain just out of reach, and many dreams die.**

Without innovation, leadership shrinks. Without innovation, successes remain just out of reach. Without innovation, many dreams die.

Innovation is that important. Without it, real success is always limited. In fact, the importance of innovation became a national leadership zeitgeist in the first decade of the twenty-first century, largely because of a widely read new book entitled *The Innovator's Dilemma* by Harvard Business School's Clayton Christensen.

Business magazines published reviews of this book, and they also commissioned their own articles on the topic of innovation. Follow-up books from many authors predictably came out, all making a similar case: Innovation is essential, but where are the experts who can teach us *how to do it?*

The challenge in all this hype was obvious. The researchers, writers, publishers, business school professors, MBA deans, and experts all seemed to agree that "innovation is the new leadership," but many of their materials, books, audios, and articles lacked…something. They were frequently flat. Too pat. Not innovative.

Too many of them read like what they were, the works of tenured academics who had little experience in the rough-and-tumble real-world battle of turning good ideas into flourishing systems and market successes. They didn't quite reach a high standard of innovation.

For all their prestigious degrees and titles, some of the authors in this new genre didn't write credibly. They sounded like the experts they were when they announced, based on solid real-world research, that innovation is essential and that it is, in fact, too rare and also incredibly underdeveloped right now in our society.

But How?

So far, so good. But things broke down when they turned their attention to the obvious: Just exactly *how* do we innovate? Moreover, how do we restore or reboot ourselves as a society of innovators?

They researched, they brainstormed, and they created numerous outlines. But most of them lacked an essential ingredient: they had never actually innovated from the ground up to deliver something real and successful. Not in the business sense. Not at the level their readers needed.

As a result, the "innovation" genre did what many fads do: it became the fodder of titles on magazine covers meant to attract subscribers. A good start, but there it stayed. It was read as information and considered interesting but seldom applied in the actual business or leadership world.

Why did this happen? Why did such a promising trend, one that many believed would reboot the American and European economies after the Great Recession, fail to deliver spectacular results? Why did it gain such widespread international attention, so much research, and so many publications only to fall by the wayside like a New Year's resolution in February?

Challenges

The problem was deeply rooted in the foundations of our economy, meaning, sadly, that a lack of consistent innovation has become embedded in over a century of status, credentialism, and reliance on experts. Put simply, a majority of these writers found it beneath themselves to promote the reality they uncovered.

When they started digging deep into the concept of innovation, they thought they were doing the nation a favor. But then they found something surprising. For many, it was downright disturbing. This inconvenient truth was simple: Few top-rate innovators were products of the MBA/professional business-school elite. They were, in the word popularized by Malcolm Gladwell, *outliers*.

> **Few top-rate innovators are products of the MBA/professional business-school elite. They are, in the word popularized by Malcolm Gladwell, *outliers*.**

They included Bill Gates, who left Harvard as an undergrad to go after innovative dreams that literally changed the world—and did it outside the accepted Establishment circles. Another was Steve Jobs, who made a mantra of seeking out the misfits, the rebels, the dreamers—the entrepreneurial types who thought modern academia was a slowly dying dinosaur and aimed instead for real quality far removed from scholastic haunts.

Then there was business leader Orrin Woodward, who has maintained that principle comes before capital and has stuck with this view come what may. They were what renowned entrepreneur and bestselling author Chris Brady called *Rascals*, "those brave souls who dare to think that the system can be improved and set out to improve it—against all odds."

In fact, these words are powerful. They are, actually, the very definition of the Innovator's heart:

> *Those brave souls who dare to think that the system can be improved and set out to improve it — against all odds*

Surprises

This was foreign territory for many of the MBA/business school elite. It was...alien. Strange. Different. The ivy/elite business researchers showed up to interviews in their blazers and the "Ivy League uniform," only to confront something unexpected: cowboy boots on one successful innovator; another time, deep morality as the central goal for a thriving and growing international business; and in another meeting, long hair and a black T-shirt. Mostly they discovered that the innovators seemed like, well, normal people—though they were doing amazing things.

Imagine the writers' surprise. "These are the innovators? The hope of the future?"

They shook their heads in dismay. "These are just regular people! What gives?"

Many balked. More than a few made a beeline back to more familiar Establishment ground. A lot of them returned to what they called "journalism" or "academia," reviewing like critics or calling plays like an armchair quarterback rather than lauding those who were truly innovating.

But they missed the point. They turned from trying to understand innovation to arguing statistics, and in the process, they didn't learn what makes great innovators tick.

An excellent example of this rebound is how many in the press responded to Malcolm Gladwell. First seen as a kind of new-style twenty-first-century guru of all things business during the early days of the innovation boom, he then became a target during the period of reemphasizing flaws.

Critics focused on his teaching that 10,000 hours is necessary to become truly proficient in your role, trying to nail down precisely what research proved that exactly 10,000 hours did the trick. "Why not 9,993 hours or even 10,071? What's so special about 10,000?"

This kind of thinking flew directly in the face of what top leaders and real innovators have learned: that, in fact, around 10,000 hours is a powerful and real gauge of what is needed to become a master in your field. The critics focused on empirical proofs, while the actual innovators emphasized the reality of what is needed to innovate.

The Wide Divide

Two cultures collided, and those with the pen (er...laptop) wrote the story according to their view of things.

This divide has now grown wider than ever. By parsing every word, every suggestion, every recommendation from proven innovators, voices in the professional and professorial business media to a large extent silenced many true innovators who used to effectively mentor others on the innovative arts.

Such business writers set out to promote innovation, but instead of learning from it, they often applied their own (employee-oriented) standards to it—and decreased societal levels of innovation in the process. Sad. Tragic, in fact, if you accept their original hypothesis that more innovation is vital to our national progress.

Result? A new kind of oxymoronic pact evolved among many in the ivy/elite/MBA business media crowd:

Call for more innovation as our only salvation and aggressively dissect and downplay the efforts of any who dare to innovate.

This wasn't a malicious goal, mind you, just the natural result of a non-innovative segment of society assigned to research and publicize the

In short, the wrong people had the podium.

reasons for successful innovation. In short, the wrong people had the podium.

More to the point, those who want to be innovators tend to listen to the wrong voices. If you're reading about innovation from non-innovators, stop. It's doing more damage than good.

> **If you're reading about innovation from non-innovators, stop. It's doing more damage than good. Instead, to learn how to be an innovator, listen to successful innovators.**

Instead, to learn how to be an innovator, listen to successful innovators.

Simple. Rare. Powerful. And that's what this book is about.

Innovation Is Vital

Both sides of the debate agree on one thing: innovation is essential to leadership, and it is sadly dwindling in current-day North America and Europe. As a result, economies that once led the world in every sector and by every measure are now struggling just to meet the interest payments on their massive debt loads—both public and private.

But the agreement ends there. At this point in the dialogue, the international discussion divides into two major groups. On the one hand, ivy/elite experts assure everyone that while innovation is essential, rare, and desperately needed, it is to be found by more effective allocation of resources within the system—on our prestigious business campuses and in the established halls of big Wall Street corporations with Madison Avenue contracts.

The other hand takes a different approach. In this view, innovation is widespread, innate among human beings, and in decline only because governments and other regulators and influencers have erected many barriers and roadblocks that are disincentives to entrepreneurial enterprise. Still, from this perspective, innovators can make it work anyway, regardless of the difficulties.

Where the first side (the Establishment) continues to put out more publications and reports declaring the importance of innovation, the second (the Innovator) is focused on *how* to effectively innovate — how to become an innovator — and, at the same time, is actively innovating.

Listen to the Right Voices

Finally, the Innovator group knows the key ingredient: If you want to know how to innovate, listen to successful innovators. Listen to the right voices. Don't listen to the Establishment.

In this book, our purpose is to innovate, as taught by great innovators. So strap on your seat belt, get out your pen to take notes, and hold onto your smartphone because innovators move fast and they move effectively. Above all, they *move!*

Are you ready?

Here goes…

PART ONE

THE PROCESS

STAGES OF INNOVATION

There are six predictable stages of innovation, and each is vitally important to the Innovator. Without any one of these stages, innovation stalls. Likewise, in most cases, the stages must progress in the right order, or innovation is hindered.

Like many processes, this is a simple progression for those who know what to do but very difficult for people who aren't clear about which task comes next at any given point in the enterprise. For those who don't know what to expect, effective innovation can feel like an advanced, incomprehensible algorithm.

Many people are talented or skilled (or both) at one or more of the stages, but successful innovation requires quality implementation of all six stages in the right order. Moreover, it demands a person who spends a lot of time in regular life paying attention to Stage 1. Again, getting through the overall process can be a roadblock for many people.

If you know the process, however, it's a simple matter of doing the right thing at the right time — and repeating. In this section of the book, you'll learn this process and how to implement the whole system by understanding the six stages of effective innovation.

LISTEN

*If we can keep our competitors focused on us while we stay
focused on the customer, ultimately we'll turn out all right.*
—Jeff Bezos

That's right. Just listen.

This is easier said than done, of course. Most people aren't great listeners. For example, this challenge is poignantly portrayed in a television commercial where a man faces the monumental task of really listening to his wife for just a few seconds.

A crowd has gathered to watch his attempt, cheerleaders in full uniform cheer him on, and a band plays to commemorate the occasion. The stopwatch starts, and the man pours his whole heart into the effort.

He contorts his face like he is sprinting at full pace or bench-pressing his best weight. He breathes hard. He pushes and struggles. And all the while, the timer counts off the seconds.

When the buzzer rings, indicating that the man has indeed listened to his spouse for the entire goal, balloons fall, cannons launch confetti, and the band belts out a victory song. The man leaps off the couch and punches the air with his fist repeatedly in triumph.

The crowd roars! The cheerleaders raise both arms high above their heads and shout in jubilation! The announcer proclaims that the man is a champion!

The Power of a Listen

This is all pretty ridiculous, obviously, and of course men and women in good marriages realize that listening is vital for both spouses. This parody of marriage is actually sad. But most people chuckle when they see the commercial. Why? Because the concept of truly listening can sometimes feel like the hardest work in the world.

> **Business leaders have long known that without quality listening, it is always very, very difficult to lead.**

Stephen Covey listed the concept of real listening ("Seek First to Understand") as one of the seven habits of highly effective people, and business leaders have long known that without quality listening, it is very, very difficult to lead.

Governments are notoriously bad at really listening to their constituents (a major source of ongoing voter frustration), only a few authors actually hear what their audience needs and write bestsellers, and most movies and music releases don't go platinum. Listening can be difficult.

Moreover, successful innovators have to listen a lot. All the time, in fact. They can't just ignore what's going on around them or listen in a shallow way and then suddenly turn on their real listening ears when they realize that the time has come for some innovation.

> **Successful innovators have to listen a lot.**

Constant Ears

This just isn't how it works. The Innovator is constantly listening, consistently gathering information—from those closest to him or her in the family, from the community and friends, from work, and from the overall society via the news, entertainment, the arts, science, technology, trends, cycles, etc.

Leaders are always readers, and innovators are always reading and also tuned in to many sources, taking it all in and making note of what family, friends, colleagues, clients, and the whole society are saying.

Real innovators listen. They hear. They see. They watch. They feel. They know how to watch the waves and simultaneously see the tide, as Orrin Woodward puts it. They listen closely enough that they understand symptoms, causes, and side effects—all at once.

The Innovator also listens to his or her gut. The Innovator doesn't just pay attention; he or she also considers, ponders, and analyzes the things he or she hears, sees, and feels. In short, the Innovator *thinks!* The Innovator attentively considers what others say and do, and he or she applies the same deep listening to his or her own thoughts and feelings.

Listen to *It!*

In all this, the Innovator is watching for something special. He or she is listening for *the need*. This bears repeating: Innovators listen for the needs people have.

> **Innovators listen for the needs people have.**

When innovators know what people need, they know how to act. They know what to do. Innovation is all about delivering what people need or improving delivery, quality, or quantity in relation to meeting their needs.

Needs include wants, by the way, because most people don't differentiate between the two. In other words, one of the most important needs people have is to fulfill their wants. Wants and needs go together.

Innovators are consistently reading, watching, thinking, pondering, and asking—all of this is part of listening. Top leaders know that listening is essential. And real listening is like "leaders are readers"

> **Innovators pay attention. They see. They hear. They feel. They listen.**

on steroids. Innovators pay attention. Again: They see. They hear. They feel. They listen.

From Art to Science

Some people are naturally good at this process of consistent personal and societal listening. For those who aren't inherently talented at listening, here are some helpful guidelines:

- Consistently read good books from top leaders and thinkers; make it a habit.

- Consistently listen to audios of the same caliber.

- Frequently attend workshops, conventions, or seminars where top leaders share cutting-edge topics and ideas.

- At least once or twice a year, branch out and attend a workshop or seminar in a field totally unrelated to your work and normal interests. Really pay attention. Listen. Expand your views. Meet new people, and make new contacts.

- Periodically go to a bookstore like Barnes and Noble and browse the magazine section. Look in business, current events, and cultural sections, and read the articles listed on the covers. Read five to ten such articles every month or two.

- Practice listening carefully to those closest to you—spouse, family members, friends, and colleagues you work with every day or week. Really listen.

- Read one or two great books, classics, biographies, or histories at a time—and always be in the process of reading this deep material. This helps you listen to the greatest thinkers in human history.

- Read Scripture daily. This lifts your gaze above the merely informational to the truly inspirational.

- If you struggle to listen deeply and consistently, set up a plan and listen to a lot more quality audios. The best way to improve your listening abilities is to train your ears to really hear.

In general, your goal is to increase the listening and creative parts of your brain and mind—to open up and hear more than what you've usually heard.

Note that this can be learned. Anyone can become a good listener.

Listen like a Leader

Top leaders and effective innovators pay attention at a higher level than most people. They really notice what is happening in the world around them because they listen more closely and watch more carefully.

They constantly "seek to understand," to truly recognize and appreciate what they hear and see. They look at things more deeply than the average person.

Practice this. In an airport, at a park, or at the grocery store, pay attention to what people really want. How is the restaurant or hotel delivering great service? Or how could it improve? Notice such things. For example, does the hotel offer freebies? Why not? And if it does, do the freebies actually matter to guests?

In one survey, travelers were asked what hotel freebies matter most to them.[1] How do you think they answered? If you said "free Wi-Fi," you're right. This accounted for 48 percent of respondents.[2] Second was "breakfast," which came in at 37 percent.[3] What else do you notice? Test your ability to assess needs.

Look at how every company does things. How does the salesperson really connect or fail to do so? How does a certain news anchor exude confidence and make you feel he or she is telling the truth, and how do others seem slick, sly, or even superficial?

Pay attention to such details. How could the speaker be more effective? How could the store make you want to shop there more often? How could the website make you want to return again and again?

Listen with All Your Faculties

All of this is listening. How could the magazine cover more effectively convince you that it is offering something you really need? How could the website make you want to add it to your favorites and return to it tomorrow?

What do the people in the restaurant really want that they're not getting? What do the customers in the hotel wish was different about their experience?

What do the people on the website wish the site would do to improve their time online? What do the people on the plane wish the airline would do to make their travel better?

Watch the Needs

This is listening: Watch the needs. Every need is an opportunity for innovation. Every unmet need and unfulfilled want is an innovator's dream.

> **Every need is an opportunity for innovation.**

As you become proficient at such listening, you'll start applying it to yourself and your own work:

"What do my customers wish I would do to improve their lives?"

"What do my colleagues need me to do that would increase our synergy?"

"What could I do that would help my spouse in a meaningful way?"

"If my boss could change one thing about me that would significantly improve our efforts and results, what would it be?"

"What are the top three things I could do differently that would be the greatest blessing to my daughter?"

"If my son could choose my full schedule and focus this weekend, what would he want me to do that would mean the most to him?"

"If my employees or those who report to me could select one big action for me to do more often from now on to drastically help them, what would it be?"

"What is the one thing that those who look up to my leadership need me to do for them?"

"What would I do if I wasn't afraid of anything?"

"What would I do with my life for the next year if money challenges were of no concern?"

These are the kinds of questions innovators constantly ask. They care about needs. They cut to the heart of what really matters and what needs to change in your life. They directly and immediately connect you with the important people in your world.

Listen to these questions.

Seek answers.

Start at the Beginning

This is the first stage of innovation.

Watch. See.

Pay attention. Notice.

Look for needs. Write them down.

Hear. Listen.

Ask. Ponder.

Act.

This may seem more like an art than a science, but it really isn't. It's a habit. It's the simple habit of genuinely listening to everything around you and trying to notice what is needed. This is the first stage of innovation. Pay attention, and notice what is needed.

> **This is the first stage of innovation: pay attention, and notice what is needed.**

Make this a habit.

Do it in a variety of situations, even when it has nothing to do with your work. Notice it in other people's work and businesses, so you can learn from them. Then start applying it your own work and family.

How can you improve in a way that will meet the needs of those around you? At home? At work? In your business?

How can your business meet needs at a higher level? More important, what is the top need your business should meet right now?

How can you meet it?

Listen…

LISTEN, LISTEN, LISTEN

Founder and CEO of Amazon.com Jeff Bezos didn't start out as an acclaimed entrepreneur and innovator. He started out as a guy with a dream.

Of course, doing anything big takes time and money, and in his case, the *sky* wasn't even the limit! He wanted to privatize space travel and colonize Mars.

With such a goal, he was a guy with a dream *and* a problem. Thankfully for book purchasers and online shoppers of the twenty-first century, no problem is too big for a man who's committed to his dream.

So Bezos started listening.

As he was listening and looking around at other hopeful and starry-eyed entrepreneurs, he heard lots of people asking questions like, "What's changing in the market?," "What new technologies or products are coming out or being invented?," and "What can I do that's never been done before?"

All of them were looking for their own niche—looking for a need they could answer better, or at least sooner, than anyone else.

Naturally, many flocked to the Internet as an efficient way to help them carve out a corner in the market for their own money-making devices, and Bezos couldn't deny the likelihood that in the Information Age, the Internet would play a big role in how things were done.

Unfortunately, using the Internet didn't exactly set him apart from others; he'd have to use it to do…something. If he wanted to get to Mars, he'd need more than a good platform for business. He would have to find a way to inventively and innovatively serve customers *through* the Internet, and in a way, that would also fund his dreams.

And he needed it quickly, since there were competitors who wanted to get to his dream before he could!

So he listened even harder.

And then it hit him! As he listened to the needs around him, he came upon another important question: What *isn't* going to change in the coming decades?

When he asked himself this question, the answer naturally came: books.

Lots of people had always wanted books, and they always would! Many people would continue to want to learn more, entertain themselves through the written word, and teach future generations their own nuggets of truth.

The world would always be seeking new information and wisdom, so it would never stop wanting knowledge.

The more he listened, the more he knew his solution! So he decided to connect the cutting-edge, new technology of the Internet, with its ease and simplicity, to the age-old and timeless human need to feed the mind with more and more books, books, books!

Amazon.com was born.

Despite going through a few startup years in the red, Bezos continued to listen and truly believed in the need, demand, and potential of his unique and innovative project.

He stayed committed to his dream and continued to do what innovators always do: listen.

Amazon became a thriving business that deals in all sorts of things, not just books, under Bezos's innovative leadership culture. This may or may not end up on Mars, but it certainly helped set the stage for the future of what business looks like in the Information Age.

CREATE

*You have to be burning with an idea, or a problem, or a
wrong that you want to right.*
—Steve Jobs

O nce you are constantly paying attention to the needs of others, including those close to you, and asking questions about how you can better fulfill their needs, you are solidly on the road of innovation. The next stage is to be creative in figuring out how to fulfill the needs you've discovered.

On a societal level, we are currently in the process of realizing how innovation is necessary for real leadership and continued economic and national progress. The growing

> **Be creative in figuring out
> how to fulfill the needs
> you've discovered.**

recognition of how important innovation is in all our advancements is creating changes in all sectors of society.

Art and Business

For example, the heightened focus on innovation has recently brought together two fields that were historically quite separate. Just consider the evolution of modern business leadership:

- Pre-1940s: the era of Independent Business Ownership
- 1940s–1950s: the era of Partnerships and Professionals

- 1960s–1970s: the era of Institutions and Managers
- 1980s–1990s: the era of Corporate Careers

Now compare the field of art during the same historical periods:

- Pre-1940s: the era of Artisans
- 1940s–1960s: the era of the "Solitary Genius"[4]
- 1970s–1990s: the era of the "Credentialed Art Professional" who lived through institutions, fellowships, and grants

In the twenty-first century, these two roads are merging in fascinating ways. As William Deresiewicz pointed out in *The Atlantic*, the emerging innovator is known as "the Creative Entrepreneur." Art and business are coming together because innovation is central to leadership, and creativity is a necessary facet of innovation:

- Post-2000s: the era of the Creative Entrepreneur

And, as Deresiewicz noted, the keys to success in the new era are networks and networking.[5] In fact, a network of networks is an excellent definition of a community.

The Power of Community

Relationships matter. They boost creativity. The lone genius no longer accomplishes much. Nor are the traditional, old institutions at the cutting edge anymore; they are too frequently shackled by administration to consistently innovate.

> The combination of individual rewards and team effectiveness is the way, the path, the Tao of innovation.

The new route to high success is networks, teams of highly motivated individuals working together on mutually beneficial projects. This is where innovation is appearing in spades—in the new economy. The combination of individual rewards and team effectiveness is the way, the path, the Tao of innovation.

This is Gladwell's "outlier" way, the thing that sent Establishment researchers and writers running back to the institutions that pay them. "If innovation means gutsy individuals networked in anti-institutional teams," they collectively gasped, "then maybe we don't need as much innovation as we thought."

The Establishment always fears the Wild West. It doesn't get on the Mayflower and brave the unknown seas. It doesn't kneel in Valley Forge and pray for strength. It doesn't trudge through the desert or cross the plains seeking for a better way, pioneering, struggling, and blazing new trails.

Perks vs. Pioneering

Why should it? It wants the perks of the old, the established, the respected, the comfortable. And it usually gets these very perks. So when the ship is sinking and a new era of innovation is needed, the Establishment looks innovation in the face and shrinks.

It admires innovation in theory but all too often criticizes the innovators. It calls for more innovation but only promotes it from afar. It doesn't want to...risk.

> **The Innovator's way is personal greatness and the rise to leadership—with all the hard work and repeated effort this entails—combined with the power of teams.**

The Innovator's way is personal greatness and the rise to leadership—with all the hard work and repeated effort this entails—combined with the power of teams. Networks and communities of such self-made leaders and their teams (forged in true, real-world performance) are the hotbed of innovation.

Like it or hate it, but if we want innovation, if, in fact, we desperately *need* innovation, this is the way it flourishes. The Greeks thought the early Romans were barbarians, but innovations among these Italian tribes conquered the world.

In their time, the cosmopolitan Romans believed the Angles and Saxons were simple hicks, but freedom and innovation eventually created a British Empire that spanned the globe. And the pattern repeated.

Cultured aristos in London chuckled over tea at the antics of backwoods upstarts daring to challenge the Empire: Ben Franklin, George Washington, Tom Jefferson? Who ever heard of these people? Ridiculous. But liberty spread, and innovation sparked into wildfires — politically, culturally, socially, and economically.

The Innovator, always on the outside at first, once again became the leader, just like always.

The world once again changed. The Innovator, always on the outside at first, once again became the leader, just like always.

The Wildfire

On a business level, this is the "Innovator's Dilemma" that Harvard's Clayton Christensen wrote about. On the one hand, the old, established big companies have the resources, systems, personnel, and advantages to fund and fuel real innovation. But on the other hand, being old, established, and big, as well as having conventional resources, systems, and personnel are the very attributes that seem to hamper innovation.

Like the pilgrims launching into the Atlantic or the mountain men climbing the Rockies, today's innovators are preparing for victories yet ahead.

The new, the hungry, the agile — these are the Innovator's friends. Innovation thrives in an environment of personal initiative, tenacity, and unfettered hard work. Add to this a team approach, where networks of such individuals work together, inspiring each other and rewarding each other in victories, and innovation absolutely blossoms. It flourishes. And it creates new, vibrant communities.

Precisely this environment was once known around the world as the American Dream. Today it is less prevalent, but where it exists, it maintains the energy, drive, hunger, strength, and vigor of youth. Like the pilgrims launching into the Atlantic or the mountain men climbing the Rockies, today's innovators are preparing for victories yet ahead.

Innovators Innovate!

Creativity is the lifeblood of this saga. Innovators create. They dream, and then they build. They face a challenge, and still they build. If they fail, they start over. When they succeed, they innovate even more.

This is the soul of innovation. The human drive to improve. The innate demand to be free and to use one's freedom to go forward. Always forward and upward.

But the Innovator doesn't create in a vacuum. Not at all. Instead, the Innovator first listens. The Innovator watches to see what is needed. Once he or she understands the need, the Innovator creates the solution.

The Innovator doesn't just do this alone, as mentioned. He or she does it as a team but also alone. Once he or she knows what is needed, the Innovator works and pushes him- or herself, going higher and further than he or she ever thought possible.

The Innovator creates by tenaciously taking the solution far and wide. The Innovator offers the opportunity to all who need it and shows them how it will help. The Innovator cajoles, struggles, serves. Then, tomorrow, he or she does it all again.

Tirelessly. If the Innovator is tired, he or she does it anyway. And he or she does it with a team, a network of similarly gutsy souls who refuse to give up.

This is creation.

Innovation Is Surprising

It may not match the Hollywood version of pampered ease in an artist's beret. Nor is it the Harvard icon of *Degree = Great Job + Immediate Perks*. Instead, it is the door-to-door, dusk-to-dawn, midnight oil, hungry, never-give-in story of grit often accomplished in a team of committed explorers. This is how creation becomes innovation.

Listen. See the need. Develop the solution. Build a team of spirited pioneers. Forge a community of leaders. Together, spread the solution by taking it to the people who need it.

Dig in, keep going, find better ways, and love the journey. This is creation. However hard the road, create. Together.

CREATE TO INNOVATE

As a young innovator, Steve Jobs was laughed out of the room on more than one occasion with his napkin designs of sleek, beautiful, simple smartphones, tablets, and music devices—known at the time as "Star Trek-esque" mini supercomputers.

Of course, it seemed reasonable to doubt his vision of future accomplishments and developments. After all, the computers, phones, and musical technologies of that time were an awful lot bigger than the elegant little realities of today.

Nevertheless, the artistry and creativity of Steve Jobs was not to be stopped.

Unlike many businessmen, he didn't build his business based on a product but rather on his vision of a future product—of what he knew such products could be, of what they *should* be. He was going to change the world with beautiful, simple technology.

That was his business plan.

Of course, when you sit down and write a plan that depends on changing the world and revolutionizing technology, you're bound to run into a few snags before you meet with success.

Jony Ive, Steve Jobs's right-hand man and engineer, was pushed to his absolute limits to make Jobs's vision a reality. But, being a visionary himself, he was the man for the job.

Jobs would frequently reject finished products for what seemed like minor or unimportant details. If it wasn't aesthetically pleasing, for example, or if he wasn't wowed by an elegant interface, or if you couldn't be listening to music—or doing any other important function, for that matter—with two pushes of a button, then it wasn't *great* enough! Time to go back to the drawing board.

While such a culture could sometimes seem a bit overdone, and Jobs certainly had to learn to grow over time in the realm of relationships, his vision and creativity were unswerving and led to powerful innovations in the world.

There probably still wouldn't be smartphones or tablets today if it weren't for the creative vision and tenacious leadership of Steve Jobs, Jony Ive, and their team. At the very least, the world today would look very different without their innovations.

EXPERIMENT

[A] dream…is more powerful than a thousand realities.
—Nathaniel Hawthorne, in *Fanshawe*

Once you've noticed the needs around you, by really listening and watching, and developed a team and created powerful joint solutions, the next step is to experiment. This is important because most people falsely believe that ideas are the currency of creativity.

Actually, there are a lot of good ideas in the world—so many, in fact, that they are too plentiful to be highly valued by most leaders. Ideas are important, but they are also frankly a dime a dozen. Every successful leader has listened to more than his or her share of people explaining their latest great idea that will improve everything!

> **Ideas are important, but they are also frankly a dime a dozen.**

Actions Trump Ideas

Most of these fall far short of their promise. Over time, leaders realize that it's not the ideas that fuel creativity and progress; it's the relatively few people who are willing to take effective action and turn their ideas into working innovations.

> **It's not the ideas that fuel creativity and progress; it's the relatively few people who are willing to take effective action and turn their ideas into working innovations.**

Such people are rare because putting ideas to work takes risk. And most people are risk-averse — trained to be even more risk-averse by most modern schools, universities, and career counselors.

But a person who has a great idea and puts it to work, ferreting out the bugs and flaws and making adjustments until the innovation flourishes — that's the Innovator. As MIT Press author Michael Schrage taught in *The Innovator's Hypothesis*: "Cheap experiments are worth more than great ideas."

How to Make Leaders Sit Up and Take Notice

Again, most leaders have heard a dozen ideas on any important challenge in their company or industry, but it is rare to have the person sharing the idea also outline the experiments he or she conducted to implement the idea, the challenges he or she has encountered, how he or she overcame them, and what he or she is currently improving. Meeting such a person makes a leader sit up straighter in his or her chair and take notice.

I've got an innovator here, the leader thinks. *Brilliant! This is rare. How exciting.* Then the leader starts asking questions to learn what the innovator has discovered during his or her experiments.

This is the path of innovation. Indeed, it is one of the vital but usually obscure facets of the Innovator that is lost in most books, articles, and interviews on innovation. Only innovators really understand this. It may seem ungenerous to say so, but in truth, many journalistic or academic employees who write about innovation, or in other ways interact with innovators but don't really innovate themselves, seldom grasp this unwritten rule of innovation.

The Pattern of Respect

To repeat Schrage's important words, "Cheap experiments are worth more than great ideas." More important, innovators turn their ideas into experiments, make adjustments, and keep improving.

Most people want to share their ideas with someone in authority and then sit back and be praised, compensated, promoted, and lauded for having such good ideas. Again, most leaders have seen this pattern a hundred times.

What they haven't seen very often (what nobody sees very often), and what immediately gets their attention and respect, is someone who had a good idea and then turned it into an excellent experiment—and followed up by learning, adjusting, improving, and making the idea a working, breathing reality that solves real problems or improves earlier models. That's innovation, and that's leadership.

> **Innovators turn their ideas into experiments, make adjustments, and keep improving.**

Experiments—what Stefan Thomke and Jim Manzi call "innovation test-drives"[6]—consist of gathering some real data about the feasibility of your newest great idea before you announce, publicize, and fully implement it. Knowing what works and what doesn't, because you've actually tested your ideas and carefully considered the results, is a key part of innovation.

> **It's not enough to have good ideas; they must be implemented. And they must be implemented wisely and effectively.**

To repeat: It's not enough to have good ideas; they must be implemented. And they must be implemented wisely and effectively. Moreover, it's important to make sure they're actually good ideas before rolling them out as your organization's next great thing. Do a little experimentation.

As Nathan Furr and Jeffrey H. Dyer put it, "Don't dictate a vision—set a grand challenge....Don't make decisions—design experiments."[7] Such challenges are best dealt with by good ideas and experiments, which teach us what works and what doesn't.

> **Challenges are best dealt with by good ideas and experiments, which teach us what works and what doesn't.**

Innovators, like inventors, don't just assume that every idea will blossom in the real world. They know that Edison had to try many methods that didn't work before he could consistently light up a room of light bulbs.

Make It Happen

Innovators put ideas into action. Then they watch, take notes, look for flaws or better solutions, make adjustments, and keep trying until they get it right. The great idea is only the beginning step for innovators, not the touchdown and certainly not the victory. And it is nowhere close to a championship.

In the book *Social Physics*, author Alex Pentland teaches that learning and innovation naturally follow "idea flow" — which is driven by a cycle of "exploration and engagement."[8] Exploration is the ongoing search for ideas (similar to what we've called Stage 1: Listen and Stage 2: Create), and engagement is the actual adaptation and implementation of some of those ideas — the ones selected for practical application, for experimentation.

Having an attitude of listening, watching, and learning — let's call it *actively seeking!* — is essential to innovation. This applies to groups as well as individuals. But ultimately innovation must reach the engagement stage, or Stage 3: Experiment.

The First Three

To be a leader, closely watch. Watch everything. Listen well. Notice the needs. Think about real solutions. Build a team of people you trust who do the same things (watch, listen, see needs, and consider solutions). Then come up with good ideas.

Once you have good ideas, or better still, *great* ideas, bounce them around with members of your team and also wise outsiders who understand the field. Then wisely experiment. See what works. Don't go big with your experiments — go little. Go tiny. Watch what is effective and what's not. Then make adjustments and do another tiny experiment.

Go slow, and really listen. Eventually, you're going to turn a few of your great ideas into effective ideas. And that's when you know you have something. That's innovation!

It's incredibly exciting when it happens. Your job as a leader is to make sure it's always happening. But hold on! Easy does it....

Go slow. Do micro-experiments. Make sure your idea works. Find the flaws, and fix them.

Never go big until you've gone tiny—over and over and over. Work out the kinks in your mini-experiments. That's Stage 3 of the successful innovator: Experiment!

> **Never go big until you've gone tiny—over and over and over.**

ENGAGE INNOVATION THROUGH EXPERIMENTATION

J.R.R. Tolkien was born to be an innovator.

While he was a well-known and successful professor, linguist, poet, and writer already, the stories we now know him for—*The Hobbit* and *The Lord of the Rings* trilogy—were many years in the making and came long after his other numerous life achievements.

This was a guy who believed in working out the kinks of an innovation before releasing it to the market and its intended audience. For example, he invented whole languages before he was willing to write the story of the people who spoke them!

He was also very particular about every single detail of his world, including facts, histories, maps, and hundreds of pages of notes and backstory that none of his readers (or at least very few) ever saw until years after his death.

Today, his world is lauded as one of the most vast, intricate, and fully realized fictional worlds ever created: the world to which all other fantasy worlds are compared.

Outside of books of scripture from various religions, especially the Bible, *The Lord of the Rings* is listed as the top-selling book of all time, and *The Hobbit* is also in the top ten, each having sold over a hundred million copies. They have been published in dozens of languages, including one of the languages created by Tolkien himself.

Of course, before any of his words or worlds saw the light of day, they went under intense scrutiny and experimentation while Tolkien perfected his innovations.

In fact, many (including several of his peers) have questioned whether Tolkien actually waited *too* long before publishing and releasing his life works, but no one can argue with his results or the powerful impact he has had in the real world.

It is certainly important to avoid waiting too long, or insisting on perfection before taking real action. However, in taking time and energy to experiment and perfect his idea before taking it big, Tolkien created an incredible legacy and genuinely revolutionized the world of creative writing.

SYSTEMIZE

If men were angels, no government would be necessary....
Experience has taught mankind the necessity
of auxiliary precautions.
—James Madison

Okay. By this point, you can probably see where this is headed. The three biggest problems for many would-be innovators are:

1. Thinking their great idea is the main thing and getting frustrated when others (including leaders) don't immediately leap in the air with unbridled joy as soon as they hear the idea

2. Going "big" before they do their homework and take the time to implement dozens of micro-experiments and improvements that slowly turn their idea into something that really works reliably

3. Going after the excitement of some new, different great idea before they turn the current one into a successful reality

The truth is that the adrenaline spike of a new, purely creative idea is often a lot more motivating than the consistent, dedicated work of turning the last great idea into a living, breathing innovation that improves the world. Some people are "great idea junkies" rather than innovators.

> **Some people are "great idea junkies" rather than innovators.**

It's important not to confuse the two. If you're a successful leader or an investor, for example, you've learned that the plans of "great idea junkies" are often a monumental waste of time, while true innovators are the lifeblood of your work, growth, and success. Knowing the difference is essential.

Don't Be a Poser

Moreover, if you want to become a better leader, you need to become a real innovator — not a poser. This means consistently turning good ideas into real innovations, as explained above.

Once you have experimented enough to work out the bugs and you've got a functioning, proven, effective innovation on your hands, it's time for Stage 4: Systemize.

This entails making the innovation foolproof. As Michael Gerber taught in his book *The E-Myth*, the key is to break the innovation down to the point where anyone — and hopefully everyone, if applicable — can easily apply it. This is the work of the Innovator, the leader, not something that can be delegated.

As the initiator and founder of the innovation, you or your direct team members are the ones who really understand it. As you worked through all the little flaws during your micro-experiments, you learned what doesn't work. And in most cases, you have a good idea of *why* these attempts failed to produce the best results. This expertise is invaluable.

> You don't want every person who ever uses your innovation to have to suffer through all the same experiments and failures. If they do, you haven't really innovated.

You don't want every person who ever uses your innovation to have to suffer through all the same experiments and failures. If they do, you haven't really innovated.

You want them to learn from your experience and skip the painful learning curve always associated with progress. This means you need to teach them, and show them, how to apply the innovation — in ways that only you as the leader can.

Write It Down

How? Simply outline how other people can obtain your same results. What do they need to do? Think? Feel? Avoid?

Write down the innovation in a step-by-step format so that your closest colleague can apply it. Then make it even more concise, so anyone in your group can do what you've learned to do. Finally, outline it in such a way that everyone can do it.

This is systemization.

Note that not everyone *will* do it. Surprise! Given human nature, most people won't be willing to follow your outline and do what you've done. As a result, they won't achieve the results you've achieved.

But as the Innovator, your role is to show them how, to give them a real opportunity — to clearly outline what they can do, and how they can do it, if they choose to.

Systemize

This is innovation. And this stage, systemizing the innovation, is vital. In fact, for most innovations, there is a predictable and effective path to successful systemization.

As business leader Chris Brady teaches, making something systematic means:

> For most innovations, there is a predictable and effective path to successful systemization.

- Communicating (effectively roll out the strategy in order to get real buy-in)
- Demonstrating (show, teach, and implement, always explaining *why*)
- Making policy (it has to become policy, the "what we do around here")

Each of these steps is essential. One team of innovators outlined the following innovation guidelines[9] — applicable for small businesses as well as larger companies. Here is our own summary of that report, with a few extra thoughts added:

- **Month 1**
  - Outline your needs and concerns (areas of needed innovation).
  - Consider the big picture of what innovations could help.
  - Discuss and brainstorm ideas with top leaders.
  - Study the research, literature, and advice of those who have already achieved such innovations.
- **Month 2**
  - More closely explore a few key potential innovations.
  - Informally talk to many clients, colleagues, and/or customers about their needs.
  - Meet with a small team of leaders and fully explore needs, potential solutions, and possible innovations.
  - After the meeting, appoint a group leader to spearhead the innovations. (In very small organizations, you may be appointing yourself.)
  - Establish a small group of diverse but committed people to guide the innovation.
- **Month 3**
  - Establish micro-experiments and closely consider them as a team.
  - Implement the first experiment, and learn from it.
  - Adjust and improve.
  - Implement further experiments, learn, and adjust.[10]

Of course, smaller and more nimble organizations may effectively work more quickly than this, and larger, more complex companies may need to implement things a bit more slowly. It is critical not just for a strong leader to dictate change but for the leadership team to take the time to work out all the bugs and get things right before a larger rollout of major innovations (and minor ones). This is extremely important!

Details Are Important

For the sake of clarity, let's slow down a bit here and emphasize a few important details. First, as mentioned, many would-be leaders think innovation is simply a matter of having a great idea. We have already discussed that innovation entails much more than mere creativity. It is essential to repeat and remember this vital truth.

Second, and just as important, some people make the mistake of believing that Stage 3: Experiment is enough. They think that if they have a great idea, discuss it with enough people, and put it into action, the rest of the process should happen automatically.

This is seldom the case in reality, however. The experiment gets the ball rolling, but further experiments are needed to turn the idea into a working innovation that is humming on all cylinders. This is the process of leadership.

As the micro-experiments progress, they naturally lead to a place of systems. That is, the innovation is so clear and so well understood that anyone who chooses to can apply it. This doesn't mean that the new process is easy. Nearly all success is the result of hard work, overcoming some bumps along the way, and using ingenuity and often a bit of tenacity to keep going.

But the Innovator turns needs into creative great ideas, ideas into experiments, and the lessons of experiments into systems that benefit everyone who is willing to apply the new wisdom. This is powerful.

> **The Innovator turns needs into creative great ideas, ideas into experiments, and the lessons of experiments into systems that benefit everyone who is willing to apply the new wisdom.**

Innovation is actually a truly profound process. When we innovate successfully, we serve our friends, colleagues, God, and other people in making the world a better place.

PAVE THE WAY BY MAKING IT A SYSTEM

In many ways, the American Founding Fathers were innovators, In fact, any time you have the word *founding* or *father* in somebody's title, it's a pretty good clue that the person was responsible for some sort of innovation, since that's practically what those words mean.

George Washington is known to Americans as "the Father of our country."

Benjamin Franklin was the Father of Personal Development and Diplomacy.

Thomas Jefferson was the Father of the Declaration of Independence.

Patrick Henry was the Father of American Patriotism.

Of course, there are many others who are fathers of something important and great innovators in their own right. But when it comes to leaving a legacy by creating a *system* out of your innovation, there's one man who really stands out:

James Madison was the creator of the American *System,* the Father of the United States Constitution.

As was the norm among the Founders, Madison had a truly superb education and a deep understanding of the principles of freedom and how to keep it.

He worked hard his entire life to continually increase his learning and the influence in society that would allow him to be among those called upon when the time came to make major changes in the world.

He was known as a walking dictionary, and he knew history like the back of his hand. In 1787, when he was only thirty-six years old, he was sent by the people of Virginia as a delegate to the Constitutional Convention. In fact, he was the main reason the event was held.

During this convention, following the steps of innovation and joining with a team of other skilled innovators, Madison and his colleagues discussed and debated the needs of their society at the time and the innovations that would act as the most effective solutions.

In short, they spent their time preparing and innovating. They followed important principles, and they applied them in new and creative ways. They built on what they had learned from the experimentation they'd already been through as colonies and under the Articles of Confederation.

The history of this event in itself is worthy of note, but Madison took it a step further. He did something that had never been done before, which has provided more freedom for more people for a longer period of time than ever before in history.

He—along with the rest of the Framers—created a system to solidify and protect his innovation, in the form of a written constitution.

The United States Constitution was the first of its kind, and it genuinely revolutionized the way governments and nations work in the world. It also revolutionized the way freedom and prosperity can truly *last*.

Because this innovation was turned into a real system, not only has it worked better than past attempts at freedom, but it has done so for a very long time, even though many have tried to take it down or diminish its influence and even though what Madison helped set up was far from perfect.

In systemizing this innovation, James Madison and the Framers changed the world.

Because of this change, thousands and thousands of families and individuals have tasted a freedom that would never have been available to them before Madison's innovations.

Under the resulting American *system,* the American *Dream* has been protected and spread for over two hundred years. If it is in decline today, as many leaders warn, it is time for new innovators like Madison.

FOCUS

*No one expects to attain the height of learning, or arts,
or power, or wealth, or military glory, without vigorous
resolution, strenuous diligence, and steady perseverance.*
—William Wilberforce

O nce an innovation works consistently for all those who actually apply it, it's time to focus. This is an essential stage. No innovation is real unless it lasts or at least spreads enough to help others use it in various ways. And this only occurs when the Innovator and his or her team focus on implementing the innovation long enough that it becomes a core way of doing things.

No innovation is real unless it lasts or at least spreads enough to help others use it in various ways.

The purpose of focusing—instead of constantly bouncing from one innovative idea to another—isn't to avoid any further improvements, of course. Quite the contrary. But future improvements are only as strong as the foundation they build on, and a series of half-baked innovations without long-term focus and implementation is a house of cards.

Real innovators have the discipline to help truly effective innovations stick long enough to genuinely matter.

Real innovators have the discipline to help truly effective innovations stick long enough to genuinely matter. Such innovators are able to consistently innovate as needed because their past innovations solidify the foundations of excellence and improvement. Over time, this becomes a culture.

The Innovation of "Things"

For example, Zhang Ruimin, CEO of Haier Group, "the world's fastest-growing appliance maker," brought a number of significant innovations to his company, including participative management and decentralized decision making.[11]

One of his company's biggest innovations is aligning their appliances with the Internet of Things, the idea that products are directly, electronically connected to each other through the Internet or other wireless means.[12]

When asked about the culture of his company, Ruimin strongly affirmed, "If a home appliance can't communicate with the Internet, it shouldn't exist."[13] You may disagree, but Haier has committed itself to this innovation and is focused on it even though there is still a market for other appliances.[14]

Fad vs. Authenticity

In the absence of the discipline that gives quality innovations time to really work, managers and organizations create the wrong culture: one where no innovation ever gets a lasting foothold, so each new idea is treated as the latest management fad rather than an authentic opportunity for increased organizational success.

Many companies have such a culture, where every consultant, executive, or leader is met with a mixture of rolled eyes or passive hostility.

In fact, this is business as usual for a majority of working environments. When, for example, the last three innovations were merely passing fancies, why should anyone get too serious about the latest leadership priority? Ironically, for this very reason, leaders and organizations that jump from innovation to innovation (without effectively solidifying each) are frequently the *least* innovative.

This is very important.

Real innovation takes root in a culture where each innovation is truly valued — and works. This means going slowly during implementation, making sure Stages 3-5 (Experiment, Systemize, and Focus) are applied carefully and with integrity.

> **Real innovation takes root in a culture where each innovation is truly valued—and works.**

Certainty

In political terms, this kind of integrity is called *certainty*. It exists in a nation where the business, family, church, and education leaders — the private sector[15] — operate the same regardless of political elections. In most nations, this isn't the case.

For example, elections in most countries cause business and other leaders to carefully watch the attitudes and words of newly elected government officials for any hint that policies will soon change.[16]

If business leaders don't forecast such political changes correctly, it can cost them millions of dollars, their job, or, in the case of families or churches, difficulties even more important than the bottom line. Not knowing what the government will do before it does it can hurt you.

When a nation drastically changes policies after each major election, the economy has high uncertainty. In such a climate, business and other leaders are loath to grow, expand, hire, give their employees raises or increased benefits, or innovate in other positive ways.

Uncertainty occurs wherever leaders don't take the time to effectively experiment, systemize, or stay focused on what is already working. When managers or politicians — in government, business, or family — innovate on a whim and ignore what was working well before, they often create confusion, resentment, and frustration.

An Innovator's Mantra

The solution is to focus. Take the time to make sure any innovation is going to be effective. Likewise, once it is working, don't just change it on a whim.

As Thomas Jefferson said in the Declaration of Independence, we shouldn't change things for "light or transient" reasons. And when we do change things for the good, we should focus on the new positives long enough to let them really work.

This is focus. It takes discipline for leaders to follow through on the promise of innovations,[17] but it is worth it.

The Innovator's mantra on focus can be summed up as:

Pay Attention to Unmet Needs

Challenge Conventional Wisdom

Push Boundaries

Improve What You Do Now

Make Changes Wisely

Make Sure They Work

Once You've Proven a Successful Innovation, Use It! A Lot!

FOCUS TILL IT'S YOURS!

William Wilberforce was an English politician and statesman who decided to change the world and then did it.

He lived during the late eighteenth to early nineteenth century, at a time when slavery was still widely accepted and looked unlikely to end. Nevertheless, changing this norm was exactly what Wilberforce meant to do.

At first, he tried to go big all at once, trying to change the way things were in one fell swoop. He knew slavery was wrong, and he knew that others realized this. However, after meeting with extreme opposition and failure, he decided to go a different route.

He decided to try to change things a little at a time, addressing each small piece of the problem before moving on to the next.

Wilberforce spent decades on this innovation and gave his life to it, and when he was finished, the results were incredible! He focused on his innovation, long after it was first implemented, and kept *pushing* until it was fully and completely integrated into British society.

Because of this focus, not only was slavery abolished in Britain almost fifty years earlier than in the United States, but the genuine integration of former slaves and their descendants as equal and full members of society also happened earlier and much more effectively in Britain as well.

Wilberforce is an example of how *focusing* on your innovation until it becomes an actual part of the culture you're trying to improve makes a world of difference in its effectiveness and longevity.

William Wilberforce was a man who decided to change the world and then did. It didn't happen overnight; real changes rarely do. Yet it *happened*. He focused on one innovation at a time and made each one a reality, building momentum toward the big result.

REPEAT

I am of certain convinced that the greatest heroes
are those who do their duty in the daily grind of domestic
affairs whilst the world whirls as a maddening dreidel.
—Florence Nightingale

L et's review the six stages, just so we have them fresh in our minds:

1. Listen
2. Create
3. Experiment
4. Systemize
5. Focus
6. Repeat

Now, once you have completed the first five stages and are utilizing a new, effective innovation with focus and commitment, it's time to turn some of your attention to other needs. In other words, repeat the first five stages.

Watch, notice, and see the needs that can be improved. Then creatively search out real solutions, on your own and with your team. Plan the best ways to experiment with the innovations you adopt. Then learn from them and make adjustments as needed.

The Power of PDCA!

As Chris Brady and Orrin Woodward teach in the bestselling business book *Launching a Leadership Revolution*, a key to success is the PDCA method. This acronym breaks down into P (plan), D (do), C (check), and A (adjust). It's a vital system. We'll discuss later how it works directly with the six stages of innovation.

Another pattern that is very similar is used by FirstBuild to streamline the innovation and improvement of product design.[18] Their process is slightly different, but notice the similarities to the six stages of successful innovation and also the PDCA process:

1.   Ideas Proposed

2.   Community Input

3.   Project and Prototype

4.   Small Production Run

5.   Mass Production[19]

Note how this follows a flow similar to the six stages. All of this is worth repeating and considering from various angles, since knowing the pattern of the six stages of effective innovation is essential for successful leadership.

Reboot

Once you work out the weaknesses in your innovation, focus on it and guide it to success. Then repeat the process.

Turn the six stages of innovation into a culture by carefully and wisely taking the time to do each stage well — every time through the sequence.

Following all the stages goes beyond mere excitement about innovation or even belief in the importance of innovating; it helps you develop as a more effective leader. You become a genuine Innovator.

AGAIN AND AGAIN AND AGAIN

Florence Nightingale was raised in a well-to-do family, and as a young lady, she was expected to settle down after her education, marry well, and follow the normal course of life for that era.

However, despite the expectations of society and her family, she lived during the Crimean War, and she felt called to help with the war effort.

Specifically, she noticed that while a number of men were killed in battle, a majority of war casualties actually died in the hospital, often due to poor conditions, lack of cleanliness, and all the tiny details that were so easy to overlook at the time.

Therefore, though she couldn't become a doctor due to the restrictions on women in her era, she decided to work with a doctor as much as she was allowed. She set out to revolutionize the field hospitals and the way patients were cared for.

She saw many simple little things that could be changed and helped—such as having nurses wash their hands between patients, making sure there were clean sheets and bandages, and helping patients bathe more regularly, even under difficult circumstances.

By doing this—focusing on simple improvements within her power—she was able to eliminate many of the germ problems that existed in hospitals at the time and greatly reduce the mortality rate.

For example, Nightingale would go in to one patient and innovate that person's daily hospital experience in a way that completely changed the patient's life—and often *saved* it. And then she would go to the next patient and repeat.

But she went a step further. When she was done innovating at one hospital, working her magic, serving the people there, and making a huge difference in their lives, she said her good-byes and went to the next hospital. And wherever possible, she left a new system of improved care behind her to be followed by others.

She would see a need, go in and innovate, and then repeat the process—again and again and again!

Because of this, she became a powerful leader and innovator in the realm of health care, saving countless lives and truly changing the world.

PART TWO

THE PEOPLE

FAILING TYPES OF INNOVATORS

There are at least four types of would-be innovators who consistently fail. Despite setbacks, they often consider themselves innovative, and they frequently work hard to lead, to implement their creativity, and to get "outside the box" and look for original, groundbreaking new solutions to major challenges.

Unfortunately, such people often find themselves trapped in habits and practices that keep them from achieving real change. Just knowing the four major types of struggles that block many innovators in their efforts can be extremely helpful. Knowing what *not to do* is one of the first steps of effectiveness.

In this section of the book, you'll learn what to avoid, how to recognize these traps in your life, and what to do to make sure your hard work, initiative, ingenuity, and tenacity don't get bogged down in predictable patterns that have undermined many potential innovators in the past.

GREEN GRASSERS

Distant fields always look greener, but opportunity
lies right where you are.
—Robert Collier

S ome of the most creative people in the world never quite make it past the first stage or two of successful innovation. Why? Simply because they get caught up in the surge of happy energy, excitement, imagination, inspiration, and originality that comes from creatively thinking about great ideas.

Such people envision a better world, improved relationships, realistic plans for major business success, and other goals and dreams that less creative people might not think about very often. This makes these creative dynamos brilliant in Stages 1 and 2. But unless they can translate their ideas and visions through Stages 3, 4, and 5, little lasting innovation occurs.

> **INNOVATOR'S QUOTE:**
> "Gardens are not made by singing:—'Oh, how beautiful!' and sitting in the shade."
> —Rudyard Kipling

And only those who learn to effectively convert stimulating and fresh ideas all the way through Stage 6 are able to lead a team, community, or organizational culture of consistent innovation. Fortunately, these skills can be learned. All of us can learn to apply the principles of innovation through all six stages.

Creativity vs. Action

Some people, for whatever reason, either don't know about Stages 3–6 or don't want to implement them. Those who simply haven't learned about them in the past can do so right now. Just keep reading.

On the other hand, some people just plain like Stages 1 and 2 a lot more than 3–6. These "idea junkies" often just want their fix.

This preference tempts them not to spend any of their time experimenting, systemizing, focusing, or creating a real culture of innovation. Instead, they'd rather just enjoy thinking up new possibilities and theoretical plans of how other people could turn their new ideas into reality.

These people are the Green Grassers of innovation, those who always think the grass is greener somewhere else. Green Grassers are often frustrated because they deeply value their new ideas and can't quite grasp why other people don't just pay them for their ideas and then implement them.

Green Grassers seldom if ever go through the challenging process of taking a good idea all the way from noticing needs and envisioning new solutions to actually implementing proven innovations in the real world with real people. So they don't usually understand that leaders highly value innovators (who apply all six stages) rather than those who just offer Stage 1 or 2 suggestions.

In fact, when some leaders refer to Green Grassers as mere dreamers or philosophers and give promotions, rewards, and trust to other people who implement all the stages, Green Grassers are more than surprised.

They are usually downright stumped and often even offended. They love great ideas, so they can't imagine what the leaders are thinking—or doing. "I know the person they promoted didn't have better ideas," they say to themselves and anyone who will listen. "What gives? It makes no sense."

Next...Next...Next...

Green Grassers naturally shake their heads in dismay and then seek out other pastures (again!) where they can share their ideas — always hoping for "wiser" or "more enlightened" leaders in the new situation. After this happens a few times, they often begin to label themselves as misfits, rebels, artists, romantics, or idealists.

In fact, they are often all of these things. But they sometimes miss one key piece of wisdom: There are also people who are misfits, dreamers, artists, and idealists who work to learn and apply all six stages of effective innovation. Such "idealists" also want to change the world in important ways — so they do the things that turn ideas into real, lasting innovations.

Just Apply All Six

The six stages of innovation are real. They work. They solve needs by turning ideas into realities. But they only work because of the hard work and dedication of those who, in huge individual and team efforts, experiment upon ideas, learn the lessons of what really works, and slowly, painstakingly, tenaciously build ideas into genuine improvements and lasting legacies.

Green Grassers can learn to step beyond Stage 2, but if they don't, or won't, they remain Green Grassers. They don't understand real innovators because they stay the teenagers or sophomores of world progress — always thinking they know what it takes to succeed but perpetually wondering why success never quite comes.

We can all learn from Green Grassers. Everyone has strengths in one or more of the six stages. But if we never develop new strengths in the other areas of success, we shut down innovation and progress. Such a shortfall blocks our inner leader and dams up the flow of our lives.

The leadership path is different. Leaders know that innovation is essential, so they learn from successful innovators. They learn that all six stages are necessary, and they work hard to improve their innovative abilities in all six arenas. Where they fall short, they learn the lessons of struggle and then keep trying. Eventually they learn to innovate—using all six stages.

See the Mirror

Green Grassers are those who haven't yet learned this or else refuse to apply it. They prefer to think that the grass is greener somewhere else, doing something else, trying yet another new plan—and that they can keep doing the same things over and over and expect different results. This is the crux of Green Grasseritis, a deadly disease that kills leadership by shutting down innovation.

If you ever wake up one morning and notice that there's a Green Grasser staring back at you in the mirror, it's time to make a change. Innovate. Lead. Do things differently from now on. The grass really isn't greener over there.

Your greenest grass is right in front of you. Just learn to excel in all six stages of effective innovation. Don't be a Green Grasser.

PURPLE LENSERS

We see the world, not as it is, but as we are—or,
as we are conditioned to see it.
—Stephen Covey

D on't be a Purple Lenser, either. Purple Lensers see the whole world through a certain skewed lens. There are many shades of purple, but each Purple Lenser is blinded by his or her own pair of glasses.

For example, some Purple Lensers think that everyone who succeeds must know someone in high places and have a secret friend helping them behind the scenes. Others believe that it always takes money to make money.

> **INNOVATOR'S QUOTE:**
> "At the end of the day, let there be no excuses, no explanations, no regrets."
> —Steve Maraboli

Still others are convinced that if they succeed, some powerful "they" will surely come and take away all the benefits they've earned. The list of such lenses is long.

Myriad Shades of Purple

There are probably almost as many shades of purple as there are Purple Lensers, in fact. The one common factor is that Purple Lensers all have an excuse for not becoming leaders, not living their dreams, not doing what it takes to succeed, and not working hard to excel in all six stages of successful innovation.

Purple Lensers always have an excuse that they consider all powerful and downright obvious. But sadly for them, few of these excuses are real. Even if they are, they could still be overcome. Most excuses are just false, flawed purple lenses. For example:

"I just can't work that hard," one Purple Lenser says.

"And even if you did," another replies, "something would come along at the last minute and ruin everything."

Yet another nods and adds, "I was born poor, and I'll die poor. That's just the way it is in my family" (or "…in my town").

One more speaks up. "Well, I'm a woman. I don't know what's wrong with all you guys. If I were a man, I could succeed. You guys need to buck up and go after what you want. I would, if I were a man."

"You're crazy," one of the others retorts. "It's a woman's world nowadays. A man can't get ahead no matter what. If I were a woman, I'd get all kinds of loans, benefits, and government help."

"I wish I'd gotten more education when I was young," a different Purple Lenser moans. "You can't get anywhere in this world without a college degree."

"Well, I've got a college degree," another responds, "and it hasn't helped me get what I want. You have to have a master's or a professional degree in this economy. There just aren't any jobs."

> **INNOVATOR'S QUOTE:**
> "He that is good for making excuses is seldom good for anything else."
> —Benjamin Franklin

A Purple Lenser with advanced degrees shakes his head in disagreement. "If only my parents had advised me to get some practical, real-life experience beyond the classroom. Then I'd know how to really connect with people better."

Another Purple Lenser snorts in disgust. "You're all wrong. All you young folks could do anything you set your mind to. I'm too old to do anything with my life. You can't teach an old dog new tricks, or I'd show you all what can be done—if only I weren't so old."

Yet another pipes up....

Well, you get the idea. Listening to a group of Purple Lensers can be very depressing. It's amazing how many excuses they can come up with. But it's worse, much worse, if you are a Purple Lenser yourself.

Let's Not Judge

Now in the spirit of charity, cut those Purple Lensers some slack if you're not one of them. Some have truly had a hard time of it. Sometimes problems really can kick you while you're down.

If you are a Purple Lenser, on the other hand, start noticing how often you focus on your past difficulties rather than engaging a current opportunity that could really help you right now.

"I wish my daddy hadn't been so keen to discipline me when I was young. If he'd just been nicer, I'd have a very different life."

"If I hadn't broken my leg in football, I'd be living my dreams right now. That one moment ruined everything."

"The attractive men and women get all the breaks. I've always been pretty plain, so I've just never had much of a chance."

Sadly, a lot of the excuses people offer rest on experiences that were truly difficult. We certainly don't want to downplay traumatic and hard life events as having no effect. Some experiences can be very challenging, even devastating, and they can leave lasting scars—emotional and habitual as well as physical.

Let's Take Action

We humbly submit, however, that people who never get past their challenges, big or little, can make things much worse by creating artificial purple lenses that color their lives in all the wrong ways. In fact, all purple lenses are ultimately artificial.

It may be true that they are rooted in real, difficult, heart-wrenching life experiences. But if you find that purple lenses are influencing your choices and progress right now, ask yourself:

Are these purple lenses helping me or hurting me?

If they aren't doing you any good, or if they are actually hurting you or holding you back in any way, most likely it's time to take them off.

Bright and Clear

It's tough to innovate if purple lenses are constantly telling you that you can't or won't succeed...for whatever reason. If possible, take off the purple glasses. Your future as a leader and an innovator depends on this.

By the way, although our focus in this chapter has been on the big, thick purple lenses that many people use to define their whole life, smaller, thinner purple lenses can also be very damaging: "I wish I were smarter." "If only I were thinner." "If people liked me more, then I'd succeed." "Why can't I be like Rob? He's so amazing."

There are literally thousands of such little purple lenses that otherwise excellent people use against themselves day after day, week after week.

What are yours?

Be honest. Everyone is tempted by purple lenses of some kind. Know what yours are, and take them off. For real.

> **INNOVATOR'S QUOTE:**
> "Never make excuses. Your friends don't need them and your foes won't believe them."
> —John Wooden

They aren't helping you.

Besides, pretty much all great achievers since…ever…have a story of facing major challenges and rising above difficulties. They literally turned those circumstances into lessons, motivators, and even opportunities. Leaders aren't leaders because they never had serious disadvantages or setbacks. In fact, the opposite is true. Take off the purple lenses!

TYPE 3

PDCC'ERS

I criticize by creation, not by finding fault.
—Cicero

To this point, we've made three strong recommendations for anyone who wants to become a real leader. First, learn to effectively apply all six stages of quality innovation. Leaders are innovators, and great innovators know how to implement all six stages of the process.

Second, don't be a Green Grasser. It will kill your leadership dreams. Take the time and do the work to really focus and make positive changes. Don't flit from one project to the next. Pick the right one, and stick with it!

And third, don't be a Purple Lenser. Whatever purple lenses are holding you back, get rid of them. You've got too much potential to let them destroy your future. (And they *will* rob you of your potential if you keep looking through them every day.)

Now let's discuss another common roadblock to successful innovative leadership. This one is just as dangerous as the earlier ones, but note that it is a roadblock for even more people than any of the others we've covered so far.

> **INNOVATOR'S QUOTE:**
> "A man can get discouraged many times, but he isn't a failure until he begins to blame somebody else and stops trying."
> —John Burroughs

More about PDCA

What is it? To introduce this concept, let's remember what bestselling authors Chris Brady and Orrin Woodward have taught on the important leadership process of PDCA:

Plan
Do
Check
Adjust

This model is applicable in every facet of life, and those who master it will naturally become better leaders and innovators. First, plan. Then do. Then check and adjust. This is simple but truly powerful. If you want to be a leader, commit this to memory and apply it — day in and day out. It works.

The Counterfeit

With that said, some people sadly approach life just a little bit differently. Instead of Plan, Do, Check, and Adjust, they adopt the damaging habit of PDCC:

Plan
Do
Check
Criticize

This is a major mistake. Yet it is a widespread pitfall for many would-be leaders. PDCA and PDCC are, in fact, exact opposites.

Those who fall into the PDCC trap can easily become chronic PDCC'ers. Instead of adjusting when things need to be improved, they turn instead to blame. Every time they Check their life and work, they see personal flaws, struggles, or things

> **INNOVATOR'S QUOTE:**
> "Stop blaming and start aiming."
> —Rob Liano

that need their effort to change—and they respond by criticizing instead of adjusting.

They blame themselves, and they blame the people around them—their leaders, their friends, and just about anyone they can link to their failures. And predictably, blame almost always deteriorates into criticism.

How to Guarantee Your Failure

Here's a rule of leadership: PDCC'ers are not good innovators. In fact, they insert the corrosive elements of blame and criticism into every one of the six stages of innovation. For example:

In Stage 1: Listen, they spend more time blaming others than really seeking to understand their needs or help them.

In Stage 2: Create, they're so focused on thinking about how other people have failed to do things right that they have no time or brainpower left for coming up with great ideas or plans to improve things. They can't innovate because they're too addicted to pointing fingers.

In a sense, strangely, they actually think that they benefit from things not improving—because it feeds their habit of criticizing.

In Stage 3: Experiment, PDCC'ers put what little creativity they can muster into coming up with new ways to criticize and publicly blame others. Let's give credit where credit is due: This is sometimes technically innovative and even creative to an extent, but it certainly undermines the spirit of innovation.

It may be inventive, but it's not leadership. Not even close. Experimenting with original ways to cast blame and disparage others is the polar opposite of good leadership. It frequently escalates to habitual harping and nagging and can be quite hurtful to people. Sooner or later, this approach graduates from destructive to downright diabolical.

In Stage 4: Systemize, the people caught in chronic criticizing cast a wider net, looking for new victims to abuse. People caught in this cycle often troll the Internet or other groups just seeking someone new to blame or attack. In case it isn't clear yet, this is wrong.

In Stage 5: Focus, PDCC'ers methodically destroy all important relationships, turn their venom on those closest and dearest, and become toxic. As caring people try to point out that something needs to change, the problem often deepens.

By this point, perpetrators usually refuse to take responsibility, convinced that they are actually just sharing the truth. In reality, they are addicted to lies and hurtful behaviors.

In Stage 6: Repeat, perpetrators are hurting everyone or everything they touch. They now likely spend much of their time searching and trolling for someone or something to blame, criticize, and tear down.

Anti-Innovation

Note that in all this, the individual addicted to blaming and criticizing others is planning, doing, and checking. But when it is time to adjust, he or she refuses and instead escalates the attacks on others.

This sadly turns innovation in on itself: all leadership traits are selfishly converted to attacks, and all interactions are focused on hurting. PDCC'ers cannot innovate or lead because they don't choose to improve or serve.

The solution to this problem, however, is simple. Those caught in the cycle of blame simply need to stop criticizing and start adjusting. PDCA is a powerful and even profound principle of success. PDCC, in contrast, is a tool of certain failure.

The Core of Innovation

When we Check, we must look for what needs to be improved — especially in our own attitudes and behaviors. Adjustments, after all, are the crux of innovation. Without adjustments, there simply is no innovation.

Here is a simple rule of thumb that's vital for leaders: If you ever find yourself blaming or criticizing, immediately stop and adjust your attitude and your actions. Apologize for any negative words. Make amends by actually adjusting and getting back on track with your true plans and life purpose.

This is a crucially important lesson. Innovation isn't valuable or good just for its own sake. Innovation is essential because it helps you more effectively live your life purpose, serve God and others, and live up to your potential to do much good in the world. The first word in PDCA is *Plan*, and the adjustments/innovations are a very important part of fulfilling your life purpose and life plan.

> **INNOVATOR'S QUOTE:**
> **"How much easier it is to be critical than to be correct."**
> **—Benjamin Disraeli**

It is vital to ensure that any innovations are serving your real purpose, not ever allowing your life purpose to be undermined by a distracting innovation or an overblown need to innovate for the mere sake of innovation.

Keep your focus on PDCA, and don't let PDCC enter into your life. Criticism and blame are the natural enemies of leadership and positive innovation.

PROUD CREDENTIALISTS

Leadership is service, not position.
—Tim Fargo

A fourth type of person who fails to become the Innovator, mainly because he or she wastes a lot of time, effort, and energy trying to find an easier path, is the Proud Credentialist.

In their book *LeaderShift,* bestselling authors Orrin Woodward and Oliver DeMille teach that credentialists are a significant roadblock to improvement in the business and political world. Credentialists judge themselves and others not on the basis of character or performance but rather on surface or unrelated credentials.

Credentialism has a long history. Many ancient aristocracies were based on the idea—the false idea—that people born to the powerful and wealthy were inherently superior to those born in less privileged circumstances or families.

> **INNOVATOR'S QUOTE:**
> "I am ashamed to think how easily we capitulate to badges and names, to large societies and dead institutions."
> —Ralph Waldo Emerson

Monarchies were often founded on the even more spurious assumption that babies born to kings and queens were literally better than all the other people of their era. In modern times, many people rest on credentials such as prestigious academic degrees, career titles, positions at well-known companies, etc.

Appearances vs. Reality

These things may or may not have been the result of excellence, but credentialists care only about the credentials—not true excellence or the lack of it. The appearance is what matters, not the reality, for credentialists.

This puts credentialists at a disadvantage when quality leadership and crucial innovations are needed. Of course, some excellent leaders and innovators have established impressive credentials, just as some have not. Likewise, some people with notable credentials are also very good leaders and innovators, and some are not.

Proud Credentialism becomes a roadblock to first-rate innovation and leadership only when people let it. But in our modern world, this happens frequently. For example, sometimes the Ivy League MBA gets the job, while the outlier entrepreneur does not. In some cases, the holder of the MBA will do better work. But in others, the outlier's work and leadership would be far superior.

How is the person who is hiring supposed to know which person is the best leader or the best innovator?

There are two answers to this question. First, start by ignoring any credential that isn't the point of the job. If the purpose is to sell or market MBAs, an MBA may well be a necessity. If the person is being hired to innovate or lead in many other settings, however, the MBA itself might have nothing to do with the job.

> **INNOVATOR'S QUOTE:**
> "A proud man is always looking down on things and people; and, of course, as long as you are looking down, you cannot see something that is above you."
> —C. S. Lewis

Second, focus on what the job actually entails. If the purpose of the job is to innovate, the person doing the hiring must look at one thing: past innovations. If it is to lead, his or her considerations should focus on past leadership. These are the credentials that actually matter to the role at hand.

Only a Credential

Every other credential is only a credential. Proud Credentialists want to be judged by their badges, awards, certificates, degrees, grades, gold stars, medals, promotions, plaques, and rich ancestors. American Founding Father John Adams called this human tendency a serious frailty.

He wrote:

> In a city or a village, little employments and trifling distinctions are contended for with equal eagerness, as honors and offices in commonwealths and kingdoms.
>
> What is it that bewitches mankind to marks and signs? A ribbon? a garter? a star? a golden key? a marshal's staff? or a white hickory stick?
>
> Though there is in such frivolities as these neither profit nor pleasure, nor any thing amiable, estimable, or respectable, yet experience teaches us, in every country of the world, they attract the attention of mankind more than parts or learning, virtue or religion. They are, therefore, sought with ardor...[20]

Adams seemed frustrated by this, mainly because awards and honors are often given for the wrong things. And frequently, other people are eager to associate with the recipients of such awards. This is Proud Credentialism.

A Better Way

In contrast, effective leaders wisely confer appropriate awards and honors for good things, the very things that most deserve recognition. In the case of excellent leadership and innovation, the credentials worth looking for are proven leadership and innovation.

This seems obvious, but too often it is ignored or put aside in the moment of decision.

Those who have effectively innovated are the best teachers of innovation, and when hiring a leader or innovator, the best credential is his or her past leadership and innovation. Stars, ribbons, diplomas, smiley faces, or past job titles (even when awarded by prestigious institutions such as Yale, the US State Department, Shell, or Microsoft, for example) are not substitutes for proven leadership and innovation—not if you need a leader and innovator.

This is an important reality for several reasons, but above all because too many young people (and their older peers as well) put a lot of time and effort into acquiring the right titles and papered credentials while sacrificing opportunities to learn to be leaders and innovators. This applies to many other roles, of course, not just leadership and innovation. But in a society where credentialism is entrenched and widespread and where innovation is deeply needed yet rare, many people simply miss the boat.

To be a good leader and innovator, learn to be *a good leader and innovator!* Apply the principles of good leadership and innovation, and practice them in hard times and good times. If you want to add papered or other credentials to this practice, do so. Great.

But don't make the mistake that too many people fall into by ignoring leadership and innovation and just obtaining prestigious credentials that have the *appearance* of affirming your leadership and innovative abilities. This is, as C. S. Lewis warned, an "inner ring" that is wasteful and hurtful—to you and others.[21] It is a major problem in our society.

And, of course, if you as an employer need a leader and an innovator, find one. But don't look at mere appearances to seek such a person. Look for genuine, proven leadership and innovation.

Outliers

The opposite of the Proud Credentialist is, simply, the true leader/innovator. C. S. Lewis called these people the master craftsmen, and he said that they account for most of the good that is accomplished in the world.[22] Gladwell called such innovators outliers.

Again, to be clear, there is nothing wrong with quality credentials. In many cases, they are very beneficial. But they are not an effective substitute and should never be accepted or sought after as a substitute for the real thing.

The fact that they are is a huge problem in our world and one of the reasons innovation is so rare. Far too often, innovators aren't given the chance to lead because the position goes to someone with the *appearance* of innovation credentials.

> **INNOVATOR'S QUOTE:**
> **"I care not so much what I am to others as what I am to myself."**
> **—Michel de Montaigne**

Of course, true innovators aren't stumped by this; they go out and innovate anyway. But they are often forced to innovate with fewer resources. And many of our best institutions miss out on myriad chances to really advance because of credentialism.

Conclusion

In summary, to become an innovator, don't be a Green Grasser. Don't be a Purple Lenser, a PDCC'er, or a Proud Credentialist. These all fall far short of genuine innovation, and they are roadblocks on the path to becoming an effective innovator.

SUCCESSFUL INNOVATORS

We now turn to four effective types of innovators. First, we'll discuss corporate innovators, and then we'll turn our attention to entrepreneurial innovators. Both are important.

For many people, owning their own successful business and building it into something great is the American Dream. This is true for people in many countries, not just in the United States. Yet nearly 90 percent of new businesses fail in the first several years, and ten years after they launch, only about 3 percent are still growing and flourishing.

These dismal numbers are of course sobering for many would-be entrepreneurs. But there are reasons for such high rates of failure. One of the most important is simply that wanting to own a business is not the same thing as having the skills needed to make it a success. There is a gap between the dream of business leadership and the reality.

A significant part of this gap is innovative leadership. Those who have it nearly always find ways to succeed. Those who don't, don't. Without innovative skills, small businesses always struggle—right from the beginning all the way until the end.

CORPORATE INNOVATORS

You must search well enough, to find the answers.
—Lailah Gifty Akita

In an article published by *strategy+business* magazine, researchers Barry Jaruzelski, Volker Staack, and Brad Goehle taught that three major types of successful corporate innovators are "Need Seekers," "Market Readers," and "Technology Drivers."[23] In many large companies, these methodologies have proven very useful and often highly successful.[24]

Need Seekers

To begin, Need Seekers focus on understanding the needs of their clients and customers. (See Stage 1 above.)

They do this mainly by directly asking their customers what they need and what they expect to need in the future. They want to know needs even before they emerge, so they can address them right away — before the needs become problems.

Stephen Covey referred to this practice as "Seek First to Understand." He recommended that leaders frequently ask their clients, customers,

> **INNOVATOR'S QUOTE:**
> "The first step in exceeding your customer's expectations is to know those expectations."
> —Roy H. Williams

employees, leaders, and colleagues several important questions. For example:

> What would you like us to improve?

> What would you like us to change?

> What would you like us to do even more of?

> What would you like us to initiate?

These are powerful Seeker questions. Covey suggested that often the best approach is to ignore complex surveys and simply ask such questions directly — face to face or even by letter or e-mail — and repeat such questions often.

Of course, he noted, the people answering these questions will quickly get tired of the process if they don't see real change as a result of their answers. But if they do, they'll become fans.

Real Fans!

Indeed, in the excellent book *Raving Fans,* authors Ken Blanchard and Sheldon Bowles suggest a similar process: Find out what the people you serve want and need, and then do whatever it takes to give it to them — plus just a little extra!

In fact, Blanchard and Bowles boldly proclaim that all successful businesses and organizations have "one common central focus: customers" and that "success comes to those, and only those, who are obsessed with looking after customers."[25] The best way to look after customers is to truly understand what they need and want.[26]

How to Be Effective Seekers

In their research, Jaruzelski, Staack, and Goehle closely analyzed what strategies and practices are most effective. They noted that aligning such need seeking with a firm's business strategy brought the highest levels of successful innovation, especially in companies that carefully research the changing needs of their customers.[27]

For example, two interesting case studies of need-seeking innovations were chronicled in *The Atlantic*. Indeed, the two couldn't have been more diverse, though the conclusions in both cases were very similar.

First, in a biting report on trends in the United States military, James Fallows noted the irony that "the best soldiers in the world keep losing."[28]

The soldiers are exceptionally well-trained, highly dedicated, and backed by massive resources. On the unit and battalion levels, they are arguably the best military in the world. But this breaks down at the national level because most regular people want to avoid thinking about the troops,[29] and our political leaders frequently engage in "careless spending" as well as "strategic folly."[30]

Many Americans now see the military in terms similar to the way they view the national educational system[31]: necessary, implemented by well-meaning people, but struggling, unlikely to improve very much, and consistently hampered by the failures of politicians and government policies.

> **INNOVATOR'S QUOTE:**
> "I never perfected an invention that I did not think about in terms of the service it might give others....I find out what the world needs; then I proceed to invent..."
> —Thomas Edison

Of course, there has been a lot of development in private security organizations, such as Academi, formerly known as Blackwater/Xe (perhaps the most familiar), which have accounted for a large percentage of the US military presence in conflicts like Iraq and Afghanistan. Such private entities have been quite innovative. They have also been accused of a number of poor decisions and actions.

Whether or not such criticism is accurate, private military forces represent a level of innovation in national security approaches that the formal military has been either unwilling or unable to accomplish.

Clearly, this will continue to be an important topic, and as usual, private enterprise rushes in where bureaucracy is slow to tread.

Like schools, a great difficulty for the military is to forecast challenges that will come ten, twenty, or thirty years in the future and prepare accordingly.[32] Not only does this demand effective innovation, but the country depends on it for national survival. Indeed, the whole nation depends on both education and national defense for at least some of its long-term success.

If school or military innovators get it wrong, everyone is hurt. Yet sadly, few sectors are as unwieldy or slow to change as education and the military.

The "Professional" Problem

Why? The answers are complex, to be sure, but at least one significant structural reality stands out. Both are run by professionals, trained while very young, promoted by older professionals over the course of decades, and raised to decision-making positions only after long, proven dedication to the current system.

Indeed, educators and top military brass could hardly be more programmed into the system. To a large extent, they *are* the system. Innovation is difficult in such an environment because such professionals tend to view other professionals as the real end users. When they engage in seeking the true needs, they nearly always turn to other internal experts.

Innovative voices in such circumstances are, in real terms, usually outsiders—or to put it more bluntly, nonexperts in the field in question, nonprofessionals in the system, people who haven't been in the trenches, so to speak. Such outsiders aren't making the decisions. The decision makers are part of the system—and not overly prone to innovation.

A second article, of equal interest, chronicled the evolution of art and the careers of artists in the twentieth and twenty-first centuries. It noted that for most of the twentieth century, the trend was for individualist artists to seek and find career success by becoming professionals, part of the "right" schools, boards, institutions, and committees.[33]

Unlike schools and the military, however, this trend changed around 2010. As the struggling economy allocated fewer resources to professional and institutional art programs, a kind of new freedom emerged in the artistic sector of society. Once budding artists realized that the right degrees or credentials don't guarantee art jobs anymore — any jobs at all, for that matter — the whole structure transformed.[34]

Now the driving force of art is the Internet, not institutional budgets. This may yet happen in education, but it is already dominant in the art community. As a result, artists are increasingly Seekers and innovators. They look for what customers want, and many of them try to deliver it. It's the only way to get paid, for most of them.

The Atlantic article labeled this shift "the death of the artist and the rise of the creative entrepreneur."[35] Where nearly all full-time artists were professionals up until the late 1990s and early 2000s, they are now almost all artist–entrepreneurs. Innovation has rewritten the rules.

Comparing the Sectors

Again, these two articles are instructive in their differences. The military has adopted highly innovative approaches to recruiting but has struggled to innovate in more centralized operational functions — especially top decision making. These are both the results of need seeking. Recruiters saw that potential recruits needed something different, and so recruiting transformed its messages, images, and methods.

> **INNOVATOR'S QUOTE:**
> "Get closer than ever to your customers. So close that you tell them what they need well before they realize it themselves."
> —Steve Jobs

At the same time, long-time military professionals tend to see other military professionals as those with the needs, so little changes.

In contrast, the arts have experienced a major transformation from institutional to individual.

Why? Because of the needs, first, of the artists and second, of those who still pay for art.

Schools find themselves somewhere in the middle. Public education and higher educational institutions tend more toward the professional experience of the military, but numerous private, charter, for-profit, and even home schools are emphasizing the needs of the parents and especially the students rather than those of paid employees in the educational system itself.

It's Your Business

How does all this apply to business leaders? The lessons are powerful. Organizations that want to be innovative must clearly identify *whose* needs they seek to understand and meet. Then they must find out what the real needs are.

Organizations that don't effectively accomplish this will lose ground to more innovative competitors. As the old saying goes, "Today's innovators are tomorrow's market leaders."

Market Readers

Another major type of corporate innovation comes in what Jaruzelski, Staack, and Goehle call "Market Readers."[36] This focus is based on continually providing timely upgrades to products already in the market.

> **INNOVATOR'S QUOTE:**
> "Know what your customers want most and what your company does best. Focus on where those two meet."
> —Kevin Stirtz

Or an alternative focus is based on making products and services more accessible to under-supplied areas, groups, or niches. The main idea of market reading is to innovate positive changes incrementally, always staying a step ahead of competitors if possible.[37]

This kind of innovation is often seen online, as websites update their platforms to incorporate new technologies or ideas. Anyone who has spent time on Google, Facebook, eBay, or Amazon, for example, frequently experiences significant changes in these sites and the way they interface with their customers.

Likewise, anyone who uses a smartphone or software is accustomed to the latest upgrade, newest version, exciting new app, or upcoming major improvement.

Read Early, Read Often

Readers of markets pay close attention to those who are innovating and already working with prototypes of the next technology or incremental technological add-on. Then they focus on delivering their version of this innovation to the early adopters, those who want the latest and greatest model as soon as it is available to the general public.[38]

Thus Readers innovate mostly in the arena of delivery — not creating the latest innovation but rather getting it out to more consumers more quickly than the competition. Readers tend to excel more in organization, business, and marketing innovations than in product creation.[39]

The lesson for corporate innovators is that sales often drive success. By focusing on sales innovations and doing business better than their competitors, Market Readers can consistently improve. In a word, they "ship."

They innovatively seek constant improvements in *process*: getting the product from suppliers and into the hands of dealers, retailers, and customers.[40]

Slump Busting

If your company is in a slump, one of the most effective solutions may be to improve your marketing game — your delivery, sales, and/ or customer service. Some of the most effective ways to be innovative are to simply upgrade the basics.[41] For example, consider the following three ways[42] to jump-start your market innovativeness:

1. Improve an old process.
2. Outwork your competition.
3. Bump the quality of your customer service.

Note again that such market reading isn't usually about major revolutionary breakthroughs but rather emphasizes consistent incremental improvements that create steady innovation. To put it in baseball terms, the best players get on base—a lot. Most of them do this by hitting many singles and doubles instead of only swinging for the fence.

Oh, and by the way, if you're the kind of person who usually does go for the grand slam—no matter what—keep reading. You're probably more of a Driver than a Reader anyway.

Technology Drivers

A third major style of corporate innovation is led by Technology Drivers.[43] This type of innovation emphasizes the quality of the product or service, the actual improvement of the item.

This isn't so much about the needs of customers or stakeholders (like need seeking), and it definitely cares very little about more innovative marketing (like market reading). Instead, technology driving is all about the enhancement, progress, and perfection of the good or service in question.

These innovators want to improve things, yes. But they also want major breakthroughs[44] that create whole new fields, technologies, and international economic directions. They want big innovations that make the current obsolete and that redefine the future by driving it.

We'll Build It...

Technology Drivers don't really wonder very much about what people feel they need right now. Instead, they focus on what technology and higher quality can do and assume that people will want it. "If we build it, they will come," Technology Drivers tell themselves.

The truth is that a vocal minority in society loves the cutting edge. Many Drivers and their customers are among the 12 percent of those surveyed who carry four to five mobile electronic devices around with them every day[45] or the 13 percent who believe that by 2024 more than three-quarters of American households will own a drone.[46]

Some nations are even trying to innovate through major technology, like Estonia's national elections held through cell phones and, literally, digital embassies.[47] Likewise, some early adopter investors see falling oil prices and immediately start purchasing...wait for it...cement companies.[48]

They aren't considering the needs of drivers so much as the fact that more driving means better (and more) roads. This is business driving at its finest—often risky but with high rewards when you get it right.

Go Big!

Clearly, initiating new technologies can be very innovative. Drivers often adopt bold personal mottos like "Live Dangerously," "Go Big or Go Home," "YOLO," "Victory or Bust!," and "No Fear!" And Driver companies embody values such as "Go Gold!," "We're Number One!," "Discover the Best," "Substance over Status," "An Appreciation for Perfection," "Thinking Five Steps Ahead," "Investing in Innovation," and "Just Do It!"

One corporate catch phrase that might make you sit back and believe comes from the Cessna Aircraft Company: "Most Opportunities Knock: This One Tears Doors Off Hinges." (Cessna also uses another pithy tagline for a jet company: "Mach. Mach. You're There.")

Another technology company proclaims: "Where some see barriers, we see bridges."

Clearly, driving is a bold approach to innovation. Of course, just talking big isn't innovation. You have to deliver. You have to get past Stage 1 of the innovative process and truly excel in the other five stages as well.

But Drivers believe in talking boldly and carrying a big stick. They're looking for real breakthroughs and upgrades, not just micro-innovations.

Powerful Lessons

The lessons for business owners — big and small — include the idea that some of the best innovations come from directly improving the quality of your product or service. This matters to everyone, ultimately. But for Technology Drivers, it is the main focus of their efforts. It may even be the center of all their innovation, depending on the organization and the situation.

> **INNOVATOR'S QUOTE:**
> "Here is a simple but powerful rule: always give people more than what they expect to get."
> —Nelson Boswell

In any case, few companies can afford to put all their eggs in any single innovation basket. Even the most dedicated Technology Drivers need to care about their customers' needs, at least a little. And even the most zealous marketing companies need to make sure the product or service meets high quality standards.

All three of these innovative strategies are important. Most large companies and their corporate innovators have a main focus (without one, it's hard to be truly innovative), but successful enterprises pay attention to quality and progress in each category. And smaller companies and their leaders can learn from these examples as well.

START UPPERS

Thinking there had to be a better way was a
brilliant stroke of serendipity!
—Lorii Myers

For many decades, the idea of the American Dream was that in America, anyone who was willing to work hard could achieve real success. The cornerstone of this dream for a majority of people was owning their own business and having the time, money, and resources to choose their own life purpose, goals, and direction.

While today the dream of business ownership has faded for some people, it remains an aspiration for many. As a lot of successful entrepreneurs and business owners have discovered, it isn't an easy path—but it is worth it.

Chris Brady and Orrin Woodward addressed business ownership head on in the outstanding book *Financial Fitness*:

If you are new to business ownership, you should know the truth right from the beginning:

Less than 10% of new businesses succeed.

This reality doesn't mean you shouldn't start and build a business; it means that you need to be smart about how you do it. The first key is absolutely vital: get good mentors! Get advisors who have succeeded in the type of business you're going to build and can effectively help you through the process....

Nearly all business failures can be traced to not having good mentors or not following their advice....

To find a good mentor, you need to know what kind of business you will be building. Then you can find mentors who have been successful in the same type of business....

One of the best books on building your own business from scratch is *The E-Myth* by Michael Gerber.

Gerber suggests starting small, holding most of the positions yourself, and hiring people to fill positions only after you have learned each role by personal experience. In this process, he counsels you to do the work of a position, learn the "ins and outs" of what works, and use your personal experience gained from this effort to write a comprehensive description of the job and turn it into an effective, repeatable system.

> **INNOVATOR'S QUOTE:**
> "The secret to getting ahead is getting started."
> —Unknown, often attributed to Mark Twain and Agatha Christie

Then do the same for each additional position in the business. As you complete the system for each role, you can hire employees to fill these positions while you work in and develop systems for other needed jobs. Many start-ups have begun exactly this way.[49]

Always Innovating

The Start Upper process can be slow, and, as mentioned, over 90 percent of new businesses eventually fail. Perhaps the biggest challenge for Start Upper entrepreneurs is that when you're building a business from scratch, everything requires innovation. Literally, *everything*!

For example, who is going to take the trash out of the office building? For that matter, who is going to buy the trash cans? Or rent the building? Or buy it? And where should it be? Also, who's going to paint it? Or put up a sign? Who will move in desks? And clean the bathrooms or sweep the floors?

For Start Uppers, all of this takes innovation. They're starting from the ground up, after all. And it's not the kind of cooking-from-scratch project where you pull out a cake mix you bought at the store. It's often the kind where you clear a field, plow it, grow wheat, harvest it, and then grind up your flour—along with everything else needed to get the ingredients for your cake.

If You Love a Challenge

We're not trying to paint start upping as all bleak, however. Some people love exactly this kind of a challenge. Indeed, for some entrepreneurs, this is what makes them come alive! If this describes you, start upping can really get your juices flowing. It allows you to build things your way and make the business exactly what you want it to be.

> **INNOVATOR'S QUOTE:**
> "If you aren't in over your head, how do you know how tall you are?"
> —T. S. Eliot

This often means that profits will be low (or nonexistent) during the start-up years, but people who love start upping dive into the lean times and focus on the chance to truly create something from the ground up. The truth is, at some level, every business once went through a founding period—a time when every decision, project, and process required innovation and leadership.

Slow and Fast

The key to innovation in a Start Upper business is to go slow while moving very fast. What does this mean? Well, put simply, in a start-up, you have to make decisions quickly and stick with them—not overanalyze every little thing. On a daily basis, the leader must be decisive and keep things moving.

At the same time, innovative leaders in start-ups need to go slowly, making sure that they get the big things right. For example, the product or service must be top-quality. The delivery and customer service must be truly excellent. If any of these big things fall short, the whole enterprise is in danger.

Thus, the leader must go slow on the big things, taking the months or even years to get the details right.

The key to successful innovation in this process is to clearly distinguish between working *in* the business and working *on* the business, as Michael Gerber taught. While working in the business — doing the daily and hourly tasks that must get done — the leader needs to emphasize efficiency. Get things done, and move on to the next task.

But when he or she is doing the big things that will define the business for what it is and will become — working *on* the business, so to speak — the leader should see efficiency as the enemy, slow down, get things right, and put a very high premium on effectiveness and quality.

Which things are "in" or "on" will differ in each business, but the leader's role is to wisely distinguish between the two and act accordingly. "In" items need quick innovations that thereafter are treated as systems, while "on" projects demand all six stages of the innovation process.

A Powerful Innovative Tool

Some people are naturally good at this kind of leadership, and the rest of us can learn — but only by focusing on the differences. Many Start Uppers fail simply because the leaders put too much innovation into "in" items and not enough into "on" projects

If you are the leader, or one of the leaders, of a Start Upper enterprise, try carrying a paper notebook with you at all times. Simply divide the first page into two columns, one labeled *Quick System* and the other labeled *Major Project*. When any decision comes to you — however small or large — write it down in one of the columns.

Over time, Quick System items are treated like clockwork, without demanding a new decision each time they recur. Major Projects become your focus.

Where possible, in fact, make one-time decisions on Quick Systems and then delegate them to someone else. Only spend a lot of time on Major Projects (or Quick Systems that haven't arisen in the past). In a one-person start-up, delegation isn't an option, of course, but as soon as it is possible, implement it.

> **INNOVATOR'S QUOTE:**
> **"Do three things well, not ten things badly."**
> **—David Segrove**

This simple division of focus will allow any leader to spend innovational time and energy on the real projects. This is extremely important. Most people—those who haven't experienced a one-person start-up and built it into something much bigger—will read this and wonder if it is overstated.

But those who have built something from the ground up know that, in fact, most Start Upper leaders spend a majority of their time on little things—things that executives in established organizations never even think about. What's important here is that these little things often keep leaders from doing the innovative big projects that really bring growth and success. This issue of little decisions and tasks isn't just a side note; for start-up businesses, it's the main thing!

Again, the key is to immediately and consistently divide all decisions and tasks into Quick Systems and Major Projects—and put your leadership energy and innovative efforts into the latter. Many start-ups fail simply because they don't accomplish this seemingly simple thing. It is very important.

Put your innovation where it should be! This is vital to Start Upper success.

Employee to Entrepreneur

The reality is that most entrepreneurs who begin a start-up come from a typical job as an employee and don't realize how important this list is.[50] They're accustomed to other people taking care of the little distractions like vacuuming the floors and making sure the restrooms are stocked.

When they establish a start-up business, they naturally do so with grander ideas in mind—like making better products or offering a better service than their past employer. With these lofty ideals, they predictably become frustrated by the need to answer every phone call and scrub the hallways each evening. These little things quickly become overwhelming to many new business founders.

This is very difficult for most people to grasp, since they've never lived it. They simply don't understand how the little details can slowly, surely drag a new leader down to the point that he or she forgets to innovate or lead. But, as mentioned, over 90 percent of new businesses eventually fail—and this is one of the main reasons.

A simple list can make all the difference, if you use it and stick with it. Two columns: Quick Systems and Major Projects. And put everything that comes to you on the paper! This creates an immediate, effective division between what is minor and should be systemized and what is a major project that needs innovation.

Of course, some Start Uppers begin with enough investment or other capital to hire a full team right from day one. But this two-list model is still very important. Indeed, it is helpful for everyone on the leadership team of a start-up.

Tool Number Two

However big or small your initial management team is, another system is needed to make this fully flourish. If you are the leader of a start-up enterprise, one workday a week, only spend time on the Major Projects list. This may need to be structured differently, depending on your enterprise or workload. For instance, maybe the mornings are reserved for major project work, and afternoons are dedicated to fighting fires. Whatever works for you.

But come up with a system that demarcates your time to these two classifications of what needs to be done. (By the way, this is an effective tool for top executives in other business models, including corporate leadership.) The one-day format (or similar strategy) allows you to truly engage your innovative and leadership strengths for a period of uninterrupted focus.

Together, these two simple tools (the two-column list and the one-day-a-week project focus) make an enormous difference in whether or not a Start Upper leader can be innovative. While the whole concept may bring a smile to the lips of an MBA student or an executive in an established firm, these two tools will bring higher levels of success to anyone building an effective start-up.

These two small innovations will, in short, release the innovative potential of your leadership and your organization. And on your innovative day, really put your whole energy into innovation.

As your organization grows and you delegate more tasks and responsibilities, keep setting aside a focused innovative day every week. It will make a huge positive difference for you and your company.

> **INNOVATOR'S QUOTE:**
> **"Champions do consistently what others do sporadically."**
> **—Orrin Woodward**

LITTLE INVESTORS

An active investor is someone who actually
lives off their investments as opposed to wages from a job.
—Robert Kiyosaki

A nother type of innovator is the investor. In his excellent book *CASHFLOW Quadrant*, bestselling author Robert Kiyosaki taught that there are four major kinds of jobs or careers that people pursue to make a living. Such roles include Employees, Self-Employed, Business Owners, and Investors.

Narrowing this down, Kiyosaki listed seven kinds of people who want to be investors. These include:

Level 0: People with no money to invest, who only wish they were investing.

Level 1: People who borrow money to invest. (Bad idea.)

Level 2: People who save money and then invest it. (Better than Level 0 or 1, but usually a bad idea unless the person really understands the arena or industry in which he or she is investing and also understands how to choose wise and effective investments.)

Level 3: People who invest a bit in retirement plans or work with a financial adviser who invests their money in various stocks or funds. (Can be a quality type of savings, if handled wisely.)

Level 4: People who invest in what Kiyosaki calls "the conservative long-term approach," as suggested by investment leaders like Peter Lynch or Warren Buffett. This consists of putting a little money from each month's paycheck into investment. (Again, this can be a positive plan if wisely implemented.)

Level 5: People who make wise investments. This is the level we'll address in this chapter. These people have been in business long enough to make effective investment decisions. They have made mistakes and experienced losses in their business life and have also made good choices and experienced various successes. They manage their finances in such a way that, in Kiyosaki's words, "they have much more income than expenses."

This didn't just happen to them, however. They have learned to take care of their finances and follow the financial rules of wisdom and success. To learn about the top 47 of these vital financial rules, as taught by Chris Brady and Orrin Woodward, see the book *Financial Fitness*. (Also see the sequel: *Financial Fitness for Teens.*)

Level 6: People whose everyday, full-time business is in the field of financial investment.[51]

While Level 6 could be called Big Investors, people in Level 5 are what we refer to here as Little Investors. Indeed, the focus of this chapter is on Level 5. Such people, who consistently make wise investments even though this isn't their full-time career, have learned a number of effective principles of financial decision making.

The Principles of Success

Consider the following investment suggestions from Brady and Woodward in *Financial Fitness:*

- Invest in yourself first. This means investing in your mind, learning, knowledge, and wisdom—and in your own business where possible.

- Invest in an emergency fund, sometimes called a "rainy day fund." Always put a little of your income into such a fund each time you get paid.

- Invest in survival preparation in case of major disaster. Don't become extreme about this, but don't skip it. Wisely consider the future, and prepare.

- Invest in long-term savings. Put a percentage of each paycheck into this fund, and never touch it. Let it grow.

- Invest in a targeted savings plan for things you know you'll need later, such as a vehicle, a vacation, a business start-up, education, etc.[52]

- Invest in very low-risk items that are "extremely secure, such as CDs, money market accounts, and municipal bonds. Many investment advisors downplay these investments because they pay very low interest, but, significantly, they also have lower risk."[53]

With these things in place, Brady and Woodward also suggest the following:

- "It is essential not to speculate with your savings....

- "Only invest money you can afford to lose entirely in speculations outside your area(s) of mastery. Only invest a little, if any, in such ventures."[54]

- Regarding investments in real estate and the stock market: "For many people, the best advice is to largely avoid these investments. The one exception is if your business is found in these arenas. If so, pay the price to attain real mastery in these areas....Get the right mentors, learn from trial and error, and become a master.

- "If neither real estate nor the stock market is your area of mastery, only put money into these arenas if you…can…afford to lose the full amount of your investment. And only put a little here."[55] While this may surprise many readers, due to the various infomercials and books highly recommending such investments as if they are a sure thing, it is very sage advice.

- Invest in what you know. Investing in anything else is a proven formula for financial setbacks and emotional strain (no matter how much your friend Johnny or your brother-in-law swears that it will be easy money).

- "Above all, never sign up for something where you are liable for more than your own responsibility. There are a number of investments that follow this pattern, and they are poison. Those who sell the investment may seem very capable, but don't ever give away your financial freedom this way."[56]

Two Key Innovations

Everything covered in this chapter so far brings us to a powerful rule about all types of innovation. The best, most successful, innovations come in two key ways:

A. Initiative to start something new

B. Innovative decisions to make something better

Type A innovation requires an investment of your time, effort, focus, hard work, energy, and sometimes a bit of your money, while Type B innovation uses all of these and also major financial investment. This is an important distinction.

Let's describe these two kinds of innovation in a different way. Type A innovation is, more than anything else, *educational*. In contrast, while you'll likely learn a great deal from Type B innovations, they are firmly in the *financial* realm.

This means that while Type A innovations help you learn, gain experience, and increase your wisdom, Type B innovations demand that you already have and exercise such wisdom. You should use initiative and ingenuity to try out new things when you are in an educational mode, but when your focus is financial, it is vitally important that you innovate on things you truly understand.

The Order

In other words, there is an order to innovation, and it's crucial. Consider the following scenarios and suggestions for each:

- If your business mastery is high in a given field, you've already learned how to wisely innovate in your field. But don't take on high-cost innovations outside your area of expertise and experience.

- If you are new to a specific arena, focus on emulating the patterns that others have used to succeed in it. Now is a time for initiative (meaning that you are starting a new thing with high energy and hard work) but not for trying to restructure the entire system. Innovate to improve the system later, when you have mastered the basics and have the consistent successes to prove it.

- If you are trying something out just to see how it works, keep in mind that you are a novice. Pay attention, and like the beginner above, learn the system that has worked for those who have already excelled in this arena. Focus on emulating their effectiveness, not on changing things. (Attempts at major innovations at this level usually amount to reinventing the wheel, but not very well.)

In short, if you are a Little Investor (meaning that investing isn't your full-time career), no matter how successful you are at your main career, be wise. Realize that you are new to any other field. When you are new, the focus is definitely on initiative but almost solely on the kind where you emulate those who are highly successful in the industry that is new to you.

Master the basics first, and only then seek out additional innovations.

This Really Matters

If you are investing, you have gained resources somehow, and that likely means you are successful in something. But not all aspects of effectiveness translate to every field, sector, industry, department, or type of business. To repeat: when you are new to something (and many investors are very new), the best innovation is to learn from the current masters in your field and emulate, emulate, emulate.

This is truly innovative, in fact, because so few people are wise enough to do it.

> **Not all aspects of effectiveness translate to every field, sector, industry, department, or type of business.**

As you become one of the masters in this new arena, the time will come when your innovations will help blaze new trails that offer new possibilities for everyone. But don't *begin* with such "innovations."

To borrow from one of Stephen Covey's 7 Habits, with a twist: 1) Seek First to Emulate the Masters, 2) then Seek to Master, and 3) *only then* Seek to Greatly Improve. All three of these steps are innovative, but the creative focus is different during each. As we mentioned above, this is very important.

Beginner Innovation: Emulate the Masters!
Intermediate Innovation: Master and Achieve!
Advanced Innovation: Improve the System!

TEAM BUILDERS

Start deep within yourself and
slowly build outward toward your goal.
—Bryant McGill

So how can you consistently bring your A game where innovation is concerned? After all, it can be challenging to always be creative and at the same time keep working hard—week after week, month after month, year after year.

In the article "Eureka!" in *Psychology Today*, Bruce Grierson asked this very question: "Eureka! You know the feeling: An inner light bulb flicks on and you suddenly see the solution to a problem. But what triggers a flash of insight? Researchers are drilling down on what's going on in the brain when the 'aha' moment hits...."[57]

How do you experience "Eureka!," a "blockbuster,"[58] a "flash of insight"?[59] We've all had them, but how can we increase their frequency? How can we become better at experiencing epiphanies, whenever we need them? In short, how can we turn on our Innovative Mind at will?

Is it even possible? Researchers studying such "aha" moments found that just one or two seconds prior to such breakthroughs, there is "a burst of activity over the back of the

INNOVATOR'S QUOTE:
"I am a member of a team, and I rely on the team; I defer to it and sacrifice for it, because the team, not the individual, is the ultimate champion."
—Mia Hamm

brain."[60] The purpose of this burst may be to get the brain to stop focusing too intensely on anything.

Indeed, the brain often solves problems best when it is unfocused,[61] relaxed, taking a break, on vacation, "sleeping on it," etc. The old-style approach of just sitting down to "methodically" figure out how to overcome a problem is often limited, researchers suggest, because when we do this, we tend to think "in the box," not outside it.[62]

Such deliberate problem solving seems to be linear by nature, not innovative. It can help us realize something we've known all along and need to improve, for example, but it isn't a reliable recipe for real innovative leaps—much less for consistent innovational creativity.

What to Do

In short, if you're going to be more innovative, you need to encourage the habit of innovating. To do this, you need to create an environment where innovation is welcome and natural. Here are a few habits, suggested by Grierson, that will help almost anyone turn up the frequency and depth of their Innovative Mind:

- Read a lot, listen to learn a lot, and keep your eyes open for new things. (The more your brain has to work with, the better it can make new leaps.)[63]

- Pay attention to your emotions. (They could be telling you something important.)[64]

- Sometimes put real focus on coming up with new ideas, and other times sit back and just relax. Both help.[65]

- If you have a hunch, give it some energy. Don't force it. Just let it percolate. See what comes of it.[66]

- Choose times when you let your mind not focus on your work or projects, when you just zone out, have fun, relax. This often creates an environment for "aha."[67]

- Exercise. This works! "Runner's high" is an example of how physical exercise can help spark your creativity.[68]

- Travel. Get away from the norm for a while.[69] This can trigger a lot of new ideas, solutions, thoughts, and breakthroughs.

- Read stories or novels. Examples are very effective at boosting our creativity.[70]

- Attend a play, musical, or other live performance.[71]

- Listen to music, go to a museum, or look at paintings.[72]

- When you feel you should do something, take immediate action![73]

- Start writing down your thoughts.[74] This is really powerful for getting those hidden or hard-to-identify ideas out in the open.

Some additional approaches that can help encourage innovative thoughts and ideas include following your dream, taking a risk, and practicing forgiveness.[75] Also, to really promote your best inner Innovator, try brainstorming and planning with all your electronics off.[76] This can help you focus in a new and effective way.

When you feel a bit tired around 4:30 p.m., a natural lag period for most people, try turning your attention to your list of projects that need creativity and innovation.[77] You're tired of the normal daily tasks at this point, but many people are more innovative at this time of day.[78] Also, take a break at midmorning.[79]

As for e-mail, it can be a downer for creativity.[80] Separate your work and personal e-mail, and don't check e-mail first thing during the day. Start with a routine that is more positive, fun, and uplifting.[81] This tends to boost your creativity.

Another practice that can make you much more creative and innovative is to get together periodically with a group of other people who have similar goals.[82] Likewise, very big groups are sometimes especially helpful.[83] These are effective ways to stimulate the innovative parts of your brain, often at a whole new level than when you try to innovate alone.

It's in There!

Whoever you are, you have more innovation inside. When you learn consistency in encouraging it, supporting it, and seeking it, your innovative tendencies naturally grow. Each of the habits above is an important part of leadership because it will effectively increase your levels of innovative thinking, feeling, and action.

Note that acting on an innovative idea or impulse rewards your innovation. Rewards always incentivize more action, creating an increased propensity to innovate/act on the innovation, then innovate/act on *that* innovation, and so on. In contrast, when you don't act on an innovation, you become less likely to innovate more in the future.

> **INNOVATOR'S QUOTE:**
> "With an enthusiastic team you can achieve almost anything."
> —Tahir Shah

So when that innovative thought comes, reward it. Even if you eventually discover a reason not to implement an innovative idea fully, at least share the idea with your spouse, a close friend, or your journal. You never know when the idea might be used in a better way at a later date. Reward yourself for every good idea, and you'll keep the good ideas coming.

Remember, no matter how good you are at applying the six stages of successful innovation or following the other suggestions in this book, consistently having good ideas is incredibly helpful to innovation—and to all facets of leadership. As discussed earlier, good ideas alone don't get the job done, but without them, you'll always struggle to be a great leader.

Community Innovation

As a Team Builder, this is deeply important. Your leadership will make a huge difference for your entire team, not just for you. So actively and purposely create an environment that highly encourages and incentivizes creative, Eureka!, "aha" thinking. This is the catalyst of any and all innovation—and therefore also an essential part of any successful team.

Of course, it's not just your ideas that matter. The ideas of everyone on your team are important. That's one reason that communities— real, caring, fun, ongoing, social, community connections and bonds—are necessary for any genuine leadership. If you are part of a true community, you'll share ideas and goals and work together on all six stages of excellent innovation.

The key is to create a team community environment where innovation is highly encouraged—just as it is in your own personal life. Even when innovations don't make it through all six stages, for whatever reason, always give high praise for good ideas. You want to keep them coming because some of them will be truly wonderful innovations that make all the difference.

PART THREE

THE PRACTICE

FUNDAMENTAL STRATEGIES
OF THE INNOVATOR

To this point, we've discussed the six stages of effective innovation and four cautionary types of failing would-be innovators (Green Grassers, Purple Lensers, PDCC'ers, and Proud Credentialists). We've also addressed three types of successful corporate innovators (Need Seekers, Market Readers, and Technology Drivers[84]) and three types of effective entrepreneurial innovators (Start Uppers, Little Investors, and Team Builders).

In the process, we've provided a number of guidelines and recommendations for successful innovational leadership. In all this, our focus has been on helping you, the reader, become the Innovator.

Now we're going to shift gears from the various types of innovational venues and focus on principles that can help people innovate at much higher levels. This is a powerful part of effective leadership, and the material covered here will help you innovate more successfully in any important leadership venture.

Our basic question ahead is this:
If you want to innovate, what do you actually *do*?

First: What strategies do you need to adopt to become a true innovator?

Second: What tactics will help you effectively attain your goals?

STRATEGY 1

GO NICHE

Always remember that you are absolutely unique,
just like everyone else.
—Unknown, often attributed to Margaret Mead

I f you want to be an effective innovator and a true leader, it is important to "Go Niche!" This means that great leaders don't lead everyone. They lead a specific group, a niche in society that needs their specific blend of vision, passion, example, dreams, and wisdom. And the key to excellent leadership is to help your niche become a true team, working together to make a huge, positive difference in the world.

Imagine that you're on a professional football team playing in the Super Bowl, and there are five seconds left on the clock. You join the huddle to hear your quarterback call the play. If this play is successful, you'll win the game. You'll be at the pinnacle of your professional and athletic career.

But if the play doesn't succeed, you'll always remember how close you came just before you lost out on victory. Not a great feeling. So of course, you really want the play to work.

> **Great leaders don't lead everyone. They lead a specific group, a niche in society that needs their specific blend of vision, passion, example, dreams, and wisdom.**

As the huddle goes silent, with the crowd roaring in the background, the quarterback turns to you and says, "Go long!" This means that you are going to run to the end zone, hopefully catch the ball he passes, and win the championship.

Exciting, right? Well, the same is happening here, today, as you read this book. Instead of a Super Bowl, you're in the reality of your life, and you're making a decision about whether or not you'll be a great leader and a successful innovator. And to do these two important things, you've got to "Go Niche!"

Community Is Everything

This means exactly what it sounds like. Effective leadership is always "niche leadership." People who try to lead everyone also try to please everyone, and this is a sure formula for failing to stand up for the right things and stand out in the right ways. Those who try to please everyone aren't leaders; by definition, they're stuck in following the crowd, doing what they think the crowd wants them to do. That's followership.

> People who try to lead everyone also try to please everyone, and this is a sure formula for failing to stand up for the right things and stand out in the right ways.

But innovators don't do this. They take a different path. The same is true of leaders. In fact, in this sense, leadership and innovation are nearly the same thing. Excelling in either of these things means seeing what is really needed in society and taking action to help people make the best decisions, which are often difficult, rare, and unexpected.

This is powerful, and it is always innovative (if done effectively, anyway). For a long time, certainly throughout the twentieth century and since, economies, companies, and organizations have generally been defined (and have defined themselves) by what products and services they offer.

Thus, as a society, we have tended to see the world divided into sectors and industries, such as energy, manufacturing, agriculture, education, medicine, law, government, construction, real estate, and accounting. Our entire educational system has followed this model, as has our economic and business system—not just in North America and Europe but in many places around the world.

Today, as the Information Age gains an increasing foothold in our society and economy, this is changing. As bestselling author Niraj Dawar put it in his highly acclaimed book *Tilt*, the leading companies and innovators of the twenty-first century are shifting their "strategy from products to customers." Instead of advertising to target audiences in the broad population, market leaders are finding that the key is to focus on niche marketing. They are building community.

> **Instead of advertising to target audiences in the broad population, market leaders are finding that the key is to focus on niche marketing.**

Groups Lead

The truth is that people are tired of marketing in today's Internet era, and they typically skip, filter, block, or fast-forward through commercials and ads on television and online. They likewise gloss over most of the ad pages in print media. Many of them purposely pay for products like Netflix where there are no commercials.[85]

In this new era of "fragmented" marketing,[86] the old-style media simply doesn't reach customers as well as niche marketing. Big media marketing is still out there, to be sure, but fewer people pay attention. When leaders appeal to their natural niche, in contrast, the "marketing" is usually seen as information, help, or service. That's a huge difference.

Dawar points out that this change will only grow, spread, and accelerate in the decades ahead. In fact, an important facet of this societal "tilt" is that in the new culture, effective companies and innovators are putting a premium on satisfying their customers,[87] even more so than in the past. The focus is now on the customer-driven economy, not the sector- or industry-driven economy.

In education, for example, this trend is manifesting itself in student-driven learning rather than nineteenth- and twentieth-century–style conveyor belt education.[88] But where the change is slow in education, it is very rapidly transforming business, leadership, and the economy.

Writer Catherine P. Taylor called this "Brand Diving,"[89] the idea that your brand is the key to continued success and business growth. Leaders who want their organizations to grow now emphasize niche branding. This entails figuring out the message you really want to spread and then finding ways to connect with those who resonate with this central message.

How Communities Sell

This also creates flow — in other words, customers who seek you out or who are naturally interested when they come across your business or mission. The new style of innovation seeks to effectively communicate the company's worth to the target niche rather than attempting to generally pull in everyone. Of course, this has long been a facet of business. But now it is becoming the primary focus of market leaders.

In this new normal, companies must know themselves. They must know who they appeal to and find ways to effectively interact with their natural niche(s). Those who try to keep growing in the old, media-blast methods are in decline or struggling.

In view of this reality, who is your niche? The answer to this vital question depends on what business you are in, of course. But the most effective niche includes people you already know, the people they know, and the people *those* people know — in other words, your virtual community.

This is the crux of niche marketing, sometimes referred to as tribal marketing.[90] It is also the field that network marketing belongs to, but tribal marketing is broader and includes many other types of groups, businesses, and informal as well as formal communities. The Internet era has created numerous virtual communities and a growing sense of connection and bonding with online and other kinship groups.

Two Kinds of Online Community

Such groups are often layered with other communities, either officially through affiliate tags or unofficially by overlapping and even interlocking memberships. The difference between these two is that overlapping memberships have few members in common, while interlocking memberships have many members in common.

For example, consider your full e-mail list. If you sent out a message to everyone on the list, it would reach a number of people. Now consider your closest sibling or your best friend. He or she also has an e-mail list. If both of you were to send a blast to your full lists the same day, how many people would get both e-mails? Which names are on both of your lists?

Likewise, how many people *aren't?* Some are only on your list, and others are only on your sibling's or friend's list. Now, what if your spouse sent out a third e-mail blast to everyone he or she knows on that same day? Would there be *more* people who would receive both your e-mail and your spouse's e-mail than would receive both your e-mail and your sibling's or friend's e-mail? Or would there be *fewer?*

Consider this repeated over and over by millions of electronic contacts between people day after day — and not limited to e-mail but including every text, tweet, update, post, and other interaction, even phone calls, online hangouts, and face-to-face personal meetings. In fact, it would even include letters or postcards exchanged by nonelectronic mail.

Marketing x 3

The revolutionary change in our economic reality is that in this new environment, many people accept input from people on their lists but not from companies or other commercial or official sources. Thus the most effective marketing now tends to occur in one of three ways:

- A person searches for a product or service online and finds comments from people he or she interacts with personally through social or other virtual media. The person tends to trust such people's comments or threads about a product, service, or company at a much higher level than the opinions of strangers, media, or corporations.

- A person hears about a product or service directly from someone he or she personally knows.

- A person is contacted (online, in person, or in some other way) by a personal acquaintance or friend and introduced to a product or service.

When there are multiple mentions of a given product or service from different people that someone knows, the marketing power of that item greatly increases. But while many companies have tried to officially market this way, it only really works when many of their customers get involved and voluntarily share their "like" of the product or service.

> **In the Internet-era economy, people don't trust official marketing. They are much more likely to trust people they know personally.**

Again, in the Internet-era economy, people don't trust official marketing. They are much more likely to trust people they know personally.

Marketing x 2

This is a very democratic style of marketing, and it is increasingly important. Indeed, the new marketing consists more and more of two key things:

1. Treating your customers so well that they gush about your company (products, quality, service, etc.) to others— especially people they personally know and care about.

2. Finding ways to encourage or even reward your loyal community members and customers as they promote your organization, services, or products.

But this can't be pat or contrived. It can't be faked. In the end, "Going Niche" means becoming part of a true community with your customers. Again, this move can't be counterfeited or simulated. It must be genuine.

> **"Going Niche" means becoming part of a true community with your customers.**

When business leaders and employees truly dedicate themselves to the good of their customers, far beyond the considerations of profit, and build authentic societies of care and connection, right along with fun and time spent together, niches become true human communities. This isn't easy marketing. It's more challenging than ever before, in fact. But it is possible.

> **The most effective business innovations in the current economy are those that help people build and improve their natural communities.**

The most effective business innovations in the current economy are those that help people build and improve their natural communities. This is the essence of "Going Niche," and it is the lifeblood of twenty-first-century leadership.

GO SERVICE

*The best way to find yourself is to lose
yourself in the service of others.*
—Mahatma Gandhi

In short, in order to "Go Niche!," organizations need to "Go Service!" as well. Going Service simply means making your enterprise—whatever else it does—an incredibly effective customer and community service entity.

Not many companies can boast such a level of authentic, organic connection with people, but these are increasingly important considerations. If your organization struggles in customer service and community service, real innovation is needed—immediately.

If you are already excellent at true customer and community service, even more innovation is needed to continually improve your bonds (just as in any significant relationship, from marriage to family to friendship). Top-rated customer and community service is the new catalyst of growth (even more than before; it was already very important).

> **If your organization struggles in customer service and community service, real innovation is needed—immediately.**

Today's CEOs, leaders, and business owners have to be excellent and genuine customer and community servants. Nothing can take the place of this vital role.

It's *All* Service

Moreover, the customers and communities in question are those in your organization's natural niche(s). As business strategists Olaf Acker, Germar Schröder, and Florian Gröne taught, top tech firms are changing in order to adopt the strategy of "everything-as-a-service."[91]

Ironically, after the Great Recession of 2008–2013, consumers noticed a decline in the quality of customer service in many if not most businesses and industries. This trend was especially noticeable in the travel and service industries, from a drop in quality airline service to a similar downgrading of service in many hotels, restaurants, etc.[92]

But this trend also applied to other industries as well, including banking, education, and health care. In fact, nearly all sectors were affected.

Part of the change resulted from fewer full-time workers in many companies and more outsourcing of jobs. But the overall cultural acceptance of a declining service ethic was also a significant factor. Higher tax rates in the leading industrialized nations fueled the problem as various companies moved parts of their operations abroad.

As quality customer service became scarcer, the willingness to pay for it naturally increased. So did the longing for it in the general populace. Likewise, people took notice when they were treated with what now seemed like highly impressive customer service from the few organizations that made it a top priority.

The New Way

The concept of "the Nordstrom Way" or the enjoyment of flying Southwest Airlines during its customer service golden age have long been legendary in business books and articles. But today this kind of high-quality, high-touch, "can-do" service is appreciated more than ever.

And since the new hottest marketing usually flows from regular people spreading buzz word-of-mouth via online comments and social media posts, companies that don't engage in first-rate, "Raving

Fans"[93] customer service don't enjoy the many advantages of being a true service leader.

In fact, many of the greatest opportunities for innovation right now are found in customer service. Every serious organization needs to make it a high-priority goal to become the top service leader in its field. Those who don't will lose market share.

> **Any organization that isn't a service leader can never realistically hope to become a true community.**

Even more important, any organization that isn't a service leader can never realistically hope to become a true community.

The Next Level

And make no mistake: Community is the new path of leadership, especially in the Internet era. In *Raving Fans*, Ken Blanchard and Sheldon Bowles teach that it's simply not enough to provide adequate or even good customer service.

> **Community is the new path of leadership.**

Companies and leaders that want to succeed must create a community of "Raving Fans," participants and customers who are treated so well by your organization that they absolutely love you—and tell others about their fantastic experiences with you.

This is not only possible, but it is the new necessity for companies that plan to grow. Another book by Ken Blanchard with Kathy Cuff and Vicki Halsey follows up on this theme. The title is *Legendary Service: The Key Is to Care.* This book shows that while many companies really do care, just caring isn't enough; top leaders consistently *show* how much they care in all the interactions their organizations have with customers and other participants.

If you want to be a leader or an innovator—or a *better* leader or innovator—turn your focus, creativity, effort, and work to being a better servant[94] and your company to being a true service leader.

In short, if you want to be truly innovative, "Go Service!"

GO ONLINE OR GO LOCAL (OR BOTH)

Without a sense of caring,
there can be no sense of community.
—Anthony J. D'Angelo

As we've already seen, people increasingly want to buy from companies that *care* or at least that *matter*. Moreover, they want to feel a connection with the leaders. They want to know that they can trust the organization to treat them right if something goes wrong.

Indeed, they want to know that they will be treated like kings even if everything goes right! They want to be proud to be customers. They want to feel like participants in the company's mission, not just customers who purchase something once in a while.

This may sound strange when talking about buying cars, lettuce, books, or clothes. But it is true. People want to feel that they are part of something, at least as much as possible.

For example, even large corporations such as Walmart or McDonald's connect mostly because their strategy is to build stores in many little towns and neighborhoods.

> People want to feel that they are part of something, at least as much as possible.

Each location is largely staffed with locals, and the managers often participate in local events, donate to local charities, and connect with the people in the area. The locations often become a meeting place for various subgroups in the community.

Connection Is King

Other organizations may own less real estate and build fewer stores but connect on a different level—based around *values*. Examples of this include Whole Foods and various organic or farmer's markets, where people who value healthy, holistic nutrition create natural communities. Churches follow this same pattern, though based on spiritual values rather than nutritional.

Other examples of values communities include scouting groups, sports leagues and their supporters and fans, high school or private school communities and the extracurricular activities that include parents and boosters as well as the youth and school leaders, business networks, homeschooling groups, professional affiliate organizations, and service clubs like Rotary, Lions, Shriners, etc. There are many other examples.

> **When people work together in common cause, bonding naturally begins to flourish.**

In all this, community arises where there is a true sharing of values, care, concern, interests, and goals. When people work together in common cause, bonding naturally begins to flourish.

Commercial Connections

For business, the easiest path to such connections is usually the direct one. In other words, real connections and community will form in direct relation to how frequently and deeply an individual or family interacts with an organization's leaders. This means that the way to create authentic community is to be in a position where customers and participants interact with you and your organization on a daily basis or at least a few times weekly.

Through history, community most frequently formed based on geographical proximity. Communities were usually local phenomena, simply because people had a lot more connections with those who resided, worked, and interacted near them.

Today such interactions are even more prevalent online than in the local neighborhood. Leaders who want to build meaningful community need to closely interact with people, meaning that it is essential to either "Go Local" or "Go Online."

Both Is Better

If a combination of both is possible, so much the better. Communities that frequently interact personally face-to-face and also have a daily presence online are likely to create deeper and more lasting bonds than those with fewer interactions.

But either can be effective. Strong ties often grow in online communities, frequently even stronger than in local groups. Ultimately, people connect where they care and feel understood, inspired, and valued.

> **Communities that frequently interact personally face-to-face and also have a daily presence online are likely to create deeper and more lasting bonds than those with fewer interactions.**

If your organization doesn't have solid, heartfelt connections online or in a local setting, it's very difficult to truly meet the criteria of community. To effectively "Go Niche" and "Go Service," the local or online community component is very important.

Of course, as mentioned above, this has to be authentic, not contrived or just a business tactic. But where the focus and care are real, community is the new leadership.

This is the target of top innovators in the twenty-first century. Today's cutting-edge innovators are leaders who find ways to genuinely boost people, not just individually but as part of a caring, vibrant community. And a lot more such innovation is needed.

Indeed, *the* great challenge for innovators in the decades ahead is building Innovative Communities—where the members themselves take initiative and improve the lives of those around them.

GO NIMBLE

We think the new intellectual property is speed.
People who can move fast are going to win.
—Kevin Nolan[95]

O ne of the difficulties of consistent, quality innovation is that leaders and organizations with the most resources are often unable to
nimbly respond to the latest needs. As mentioned before, identi-
fying needs and then rising to the challenge of turning them into opportunities is really what innovation is all about. But too often those
with the most potential to help meet the newest and greatest needs
lack the ability to quickly change direction and deal with what is most
needed right now.

This is the struggle of institutionalism. As institutions become
bigger and more reliant on bureaucratic systems and standard
operating procedures, they often find it difficult to nimbly shift gears
to deal with every new community need.

Institutionalism

A significant role for real leaders is growing while remaining
nimble, creating a nimble system of innovation.[96] If your organization
is small, now is the time to start. Stay nimble, and make it a value.
Then as you grow, make sure to maintain this priority. This will, of
course, require consistent innovation on your part as a leader.

If you are already leading a large entity that is community-
responsive and nimble, the challenge is to keep it this way. Again, in

such circumstances, innovation is key. Or perhaps you are a leader in a big institution that hasn't cultivated an imperative to remain nimble; you may never have really valued this important trait. If so, your work is cut out for you. To succeed in the new economy, being nimble is essential—because it is an inherent characteristic of genuine communities.

In fact, not being nimble is a direct announcement to the world that your organization doesn't truly value community. Why? Because to effectively help any community over time, an institution must be able to assess and respond to its needs—when they arise and in time to actually address them. Being agile and authentically responsive is the only way to truly be responsible and available.

Being nimble is part of leadership nowadays.

This is profound, actually. It's the essence of what Jim Collins called the shift from "Good to Great" companies. When you as a leader are genuinely innovative, you build an organization that is effectively nimble—thus becoming an intricate part of the community and a leading source of community success and progress.

> **Being agile and authentically responsive is the only way to truly be responsible and available.**

Without the choice to be agile, innovation seldom really connects. But when you are nimble, it almost always makes a real difference. Go Nimble!

GO DEEP

*I alone cannot change the world, but I can cast a stone
across the water to create many ripples.*
—Unknown, often attributed to Mother Teresa

A fifth strategy of quality, effective innovation is to "Go Deep!" This combines the earlier four strategies [Go Niche, Go Service, Go Online or Go Local (or both), and Go Nimble] and elevates them all to a higher plane. In other words, instead of just repeating or adjusting in order to spread needed innovations, the top leader helps make innovating a part of the culture itself.

"Going Deep" means getting the spirit of innovation all through every part of your business or organization. This is important but not always easy.

There are, in fact, many ways to "Go Deep!" There are as many ways to do this as there are innovative leaders and needs that demand innovations.

The best leaders encourage and reward innovation throughout the organization. Top leaders also teach their people to teach everyone they lead to innovate and to keep teaching anyone who joins their community the same thing. This creates the truly innovative culture.

In this sense, everyone can and should become the Innovator.

> **Top leaders not only innovate; they teach their people to innovate, and they encourage and reward innovation throughout the organization.**

The Innovative Organization

This is deep. The Innovator always creates an innovative organization and, on the broader scale, an innovative community.

> The Innovator always creates an innovative organization and, on the broader scale, an innovative community.

Such communities naturally influence the even larger society. This increases the value of innovation and makes it more of a cultural phenomenon.

Again, this is the definition of "Going Deep!" And it brings us full circle. Remember picturing yourself in the huddle at the Super Bowl, being told by the quarterback to "Go Deep" and win the championship? That's what doing all five of these strategies will accomplish—not in a literal football game but in the victory of being the Innovator and helping many others do the same.

This doesn't just benefit you or your business. It builds community, spreads leadership, and infuses the culture of our society with more and more desire to truly innovate—to address real needs in exciting, effective, innovative ways that bring significant progress.

Indeed, this is the legacy of the Innovator. Success is always part of progress! When you build and lead a team of highly successful, innovative leaders, it has a direct and lasting influence on the progress of the community and—if you keep at it long enough and well enough—on the society as a whole.

Success and Progress

Again, there is no real progress (in society or organizations) without serious success (the achievements of individuals and teams). Your victories and the victories of the people you lead are a powerful step toward community and societal victory. The best business leaders naturally spread leadership to deal with the needs of a nation. Orrin Woodward and Oliver DeMille called this a "LeaderShift," where excellent business leadership spurs and contributes to major national improvements and progress.

But it all starts with the initiative of the Innovator. That means *you* and everyone on your team and in your organization.

When you engage the six stages of effective innovation and add to these the five strategies we've just covered, you naturally "Go Deep." This takes your innovations far and wide, especially when you teach everyone you influence to become the Innovator — and help everyone they influence to do the same.

Spreading Ripples

Stephen Covey called this "Being Proactive" and listed it as the *first* habit of highly effective people.[97] When we are truly proactive, we take initiative, we innovate, and we help others do the same. Covey likened this to a drop falling in a pool of water, creating ripples that spread far beyond the original action.

The ripples of your effective innovations will make a significant difference in the lives of many people. And as you teach others to be excellent innovative leaders as well, the ripples will be too many to count. Go Deep!

There is nothing that can take the place of this approach. When you build a team of innovative leaders going deep, you're literally fixing the world — one person and one community at a time. This is the path of the explorer, the discoverer, the trailblazer, the pioneer, the guide, the founding father or mother, the great leader.

> **When you build a team of innovative leaders going deep, you're literally fixing the world— one person and one community at a time.**

BASIC TACTICS OF INNOVATION

There. The strategy is set: Go Niche! Go Service! Go Local or Go Online (or both)! Go Nimble! And Go Deep!

But a strategy is only as good as the tactics that turn it into a reality — the daily application, the work, the adjustments, the people, the effort, and the choice to keep going and keep improving. This is where the rubber meets the road.

Here you encounter the sometimes gut-wrenching decision to never give up, even in the face of great challenges, and the daily choice to keep working, working, working. This is the blue-collar, lunch-bucket reality of what either gets done or doesn't.

In every arena of endeavor, the tactics and the follow-through determine ultimate outcomes. The results are sure, depending on the actions — especially those that must be repeated, day after day, week after week, until victory is attained. It is the little things, the small things, done over and over and over, that make the real difference.

Of course, doing them is essential. But getting them right, so that you do the right "little things" over and over, is simply vital. Without that, success remains ever elusive, always a mirage. But when you know the right things to do and how to do them correctly, the rest is up to you.

Here we discuss the tactics of quality innovation, those things that must be done right and done often with focused intensity and consistency.

When you do them, success is sure. But first, you must know what to do....

TACTIC 1

THE BRAINSTORM

If you wish to advance into the infinite,
explore the finite in all directions.
—Johann Wolfgang von Goethe

Sometimes innovative ideas come during the heat of your work, but at other times you have to sit down, ponder, and think. In fact, thinking can be very hard work. It is essential to give yourself time to think innovatively. And like almost any other work that matters, this is most effective when you have a set time to focus on it.

In other words, set aside a specific time each week to brainstorm. This creates a structure in your life that is conducive to creativity and innovational thinking. Top leaders know that to do something effectively, they need to focus on it, and they need to do so consistently.

But this doesn't mean you can't do anything else. In your busy life, you'll need to do a lot of other things. The truth is that people who only sit around trying to be innovative aren't as creative as those who do it while they pursue other important tasks, relationships, and projects. But a little focused time *is* needed. And if it is consistent, you'll become an innovative leader.

> **Top leaders know that to do something effectively, they need to focus on it, and they need to do so consistently.**

Set a Time

Many top leaders have a creative brainstorm once a week. They may do it more often, when a lot of innovative ideas are flowing for whatever reason, but they make sure to set aside some time every week to focus on brainstorming ways to improve their work, family, and life.

This is usually most effective when it's done at the same time each week. For some people, the best time is Sunday evening, for others it is early Monday morning, and for still others, the most effective time may be Thursday at 10:00 a.m. — whatever works well for their specific schedule.

Consider the best time for you, and perhaps even try a few options to see what works. But come up with a specific time in the week where you can put aside everything else, ponder deeply, and brainstorm.

Make It Real: Put It on Paper

A key to effective brainstorming is to write down the ideas you come up with. In fact, it helps to have a brainstorm notebook dedicated to this process. This allows you to start each week's meeting with a review of past ideas that you haven't yet fully implemented. It can get your creativity flowing, and then when you turn to a new page for this week's ideas, you're already in the innovative mode.

> **Too many excellent innovations are lost because the idea comes at night but is forgotten by morning.**

It's a good idea to keep this notebook near your bed as well so that if you have a great idea during the night, you can quickly write it down. Too many excellent innovations are lost because the idea comes at night but is forgotten by morning. You remember you had a great idea during the night, but you just can't recall what it was.

Write each idea down, whether at night or at any point during the day. Also, it is more effective to write ideas out by hand than to type them. The hand movements in writing are tied to muscle memory, and people tend to remember better after handwriting an idea than they do after typing one.

Also, handwriting your ideas gives you greater flexibility on the page: you can draw arrows, doodle a picture or diagram, cross something out easily (so that it's still there if you want it back later), and keep it all in one easy-to-carry place. If this is the technique of choice for Jony Ive, Apple's lead industrial designer, then it's probably good enough for the rest of us.

As you brainstorm each week, or anytime the need arises, open your notebook and review past entries. Then turn to a new page, and write your topic at the top. If necessary, you can write several topics at the top of multiple pages and skip between them as ideas come.

Brainstorming

There are several effective techniques of brainstorming. One way to get the ideas flowing is simple Brainstorming, as we've already mentioned. To do this, focus on a task, project, challenge, system, or opportunity, and start with a question, such as "How could we make this challenge into a huge positive for us?" or "In what ways can we make this process much better?" Asking good questions is a key.

Then write down every idea that comes. Don't analyze the ideas at this point. Too much analysis at the wrong time causes a creative paralysis, meaning that your creativity shuts down when everything you think of gets attacked by your pragmatic side.

> **Too much analysis at the wrong time causes a creative paralysis, meaning that your creativity shuts down when everything you think of gets attacked by your pragmatic side.**

You'll have time to analyze the pros and cons of each idea later. During the brainstorm, just focus on ideas—and get as many as possible on your paper.

Top leaders who don't brainstorm frequently and consistently will lose their edge. They won't remain top leaders for long because innovation is essential to continued progress and success. Keep brainstorming, and make it an official, focused weekly event.

Treat your brainstorming meeting the way you would a meeting with a very important person—because that's exactly what it is. If you have to reschedule, do so formally, with a specific time and place. Then follow through. Don't miss this essential meeting with yourself.

> **Top leaders who don't brainstorm frequently and consistently will lose their edge.**

PeopleStorming

A second kind is PeopleStorming, where you brainstorm help for a certain person or group. To do this, simply write the individual or group name at the top of your page, and ask yourself, "What can I do to help Johnny?," "What can I do to help the executive team?," "What does the executive team (or Johnny) need right now?," etc.

Then write down every thought that comes to mind, without analyzing it. Get every idea on paper, and analyze it later. And remember to keep your notes. Some of the ideas that don't get used right away might be the perfect thing later on. Keep them close to you in your innovation notebook, and refer to the notebook each week when you sit to brainstorm.

PeopleStorming is especially valuable to top leaders because most of the time, major challenges and also significant opportunities are closely connected with a person or group of people. Focusing on the right people and what they need, rather than getting sidetracked on tasks or emotions, is more conducive to creativity and innovation.

Storyboarding

Another kind of brainstorming comes when you create a storyboard for your ideas. To do this, simply put the person, project, challenge, or opportunity at the top of your page, and ask your key question: "What does this group most need right now?" or "How can we make this problem into an excellent improvement?"

Then draw a circle in the middle of your page or board, and write your first idea for success inside the circle. Again, this is much more effective with handwriting than typing.

Once you have your idea written in the circle, draw a line from the circle to another circle, and write down any ideas that are related. Draw four or five circles on lines out from the center circle, and fill them with ideas on how to improve things. The goal is to get a cluster of ideas on how to deal with the situation. Diagram your thoughts. You can write all of your ideas on sticky notes or cards that you tape or pin on the board so you will have even greater flexibility to quickly and easily reorganize or rearrange your ideas later.

Then, draw additional lines from all the new circles you've made, and create clusters of ideas about these thoughts as well. And as you're going, if any unrelated idea comes up, draw a new circle somewhere on the page, and start a cluster for that thought. Get as many clusters of ideas on the page as possible, and use multiple pages.

If the sequence of the material is a top consideration, arranging the ideas in columns of subtopics instead of clusters of circles can be very effective and helpful with organizing ideas later when you get to that stage. Don't do any analysis yet; just get your ideas out of your head and onto the page. This is a powerful way to tap into your subconscious mind and bring hidden or even half-formed thoughts into the light of day.

Keep adding new ideas until you realize that you've got some real answers to whatever your innovative needs are right now. And even then, add a few more clusters before you quit.

Color Outside the Lines

Those last few ideas are often some of the most imaginative and innovative because once your brain realizes that innovation is the goal and starts doing it, you tap into your best creativity.

You may even end up writing a few clusters or pages of clusters on other topics that you didn't plan to brainstorm. That's excellent because innovation isn't usually tidy or governed by strict rules. The whole point is to think outside the box and color outside the lines. If you're not doing so, you're not really innovating.

So let the clusters roll, and see where they take you. If an idea comes, draw a quick circle, and write the new idea down inside the circle. Then draw lines and other circles, and see what creative ideas you can add to the cluster and what other clusters you can add to the page.

> **The whole point is to think outside the box and color outside the lines. If you're not doing so, you're not really innovating.**

Once you do this a few times, you'll likely become very good at using this tool to get good ideas out of your hidden brain areas and onto paper, where you can use them. In fact, the harder this process is for you at first, the more you need it! If it's a struggle, then you've likely been hiding some really good ideas for a long time.

That's good news, because it means you've got some excellent innovations hidden away inside. Start getting them out in clusters, and keep at it until you're really good at this.

The great ideas will come. And then, once you're skilled at this process, keep using it — weekly, at a set time — to bring more creativity and innovation to your efforts, work, relationships, and leadership. This is an excellent skill for top leaders.

Vision Boarding

If you hit a roadblock and just can't seem to come up with the innovative ideas you need, try going an extra step beyond Brainstorming or Storyboarding. Get a large piece of wood or construction paper or even a medium-size white board or corkboard, and post pictures on it. This is called Vision Boarding, and it can be powerful because it moves your mind past current issues and gets you focusing on dreams, goals, and what you really want.

Get a pile of magazines—a bunch of different types—and start going through them. There is something strongly evocative about images. Cut out anything that strikes you: a car, a person jogging to get into better shape, a saying or sentence that is inspiring, a trip to Hawaii, or whatever else you see in a magazine that makes you feel something special.

Cut it out, and glue, tape, or tack it up on your board. Then upgrade your board when you come across something else you really want. Keep the board near your desk or work area at home, and look at it often. It's fun, and it keeps your mind focused on what you want.

Focus on putting pictures and phrases on your vision board that create the right kind of emotions every time you glance at them. This is a powerful support to your innovational brain and to other parts of your psyche as well (such as the "hard work" center and the "never give up" place in your heart). The vision board helps you align your emotions with your goals and plans.

Vision Boarding can help you jump-start your creativity when you're struggling to be innovative. Once you've got a number of images posted on your board, pull out your brainstorming notebook and ask, "How can I get the _____ on my vision board? What do I need to do? In what ways can I make it a reality?"

> **The vision board helps you align your emotions with your goals and plans.**

Then start writing things down, either through traditional Brainstorming or in one of the other ways, like Storyboarding or PeopleStorming, to help your team and colleagues really step things up. As you do this, look up at the vision board occasionally, and let your emotions help the whole process.

Storyboarding and Vision Boarding Really Work

As one account shared:

Leadership author John Assaraf tells the story of visualizing what he wanted in his life. He created a storyboard by cutting out pictures of what he wanted and posting them on a board that he looked at every day. He knew the power of change through visualization, and he put it to work.

In the process, he cut out a picture of a house he really liked. Each day he looked at this picture on his board and told himself that someday he wanted a house just like it. This daily process influenced his choices, and his business grew.

Years later, after moving his family to a new home, John was unpacking boxes in his office and came across his old storyboard — with pictures of things he had wanted years before still taped onto it. When he looked at the magazine cutout of the house on the storyboard, he was shocked. He took the picture down and walked outside to make sure.

> **Storyboards and vision boards can be very effective because they help create alignment between your work and goals and also your dreams and vision.**

He found that he had, in fact, unknowingly just purchased and moved into the exact house from the picture. Not a house "like" it, but the exact same house.[98]

Storyboards and vision boards can be very effective because they help create alignment between your work and goals and also your dreams and vision. This is a profound level of brainstorming, and it can help you overcome blocks in your creativity and innovation.

Horizon Brainstorming

Another way to boost your brainstorming to increased innovation and creativity in your weekly brainstorm session is to engage the "horizon." This consists of changing the way you brainstorm in some slight but significant ways.

First, turn your notebook sideways so the long part of the page is horizontal. Then draw a horizon across the page.

Once you have the horizon, start by writing down a few things you think are ahead of you in your life. Begin with the immediate future, then things that are coming soon, and then things that are just over the horizon for you in the months and years ahead.

This puts your brainstorm in a temporal or timeline context so that time is an important element of your innovation. Once this is on the page (a horizon and a list of a few things you think are coming), switch to another color pen, and begin writing the ideas you have for how to create the best, most exciting and excellent future you can.

You can put them at the bottom of the page if you think they are immediate, higher on the page — near the horizon — if you feel they are a ways off, or above the horizon if they won't come for a year or more. Just make sure to write them down.

Keep asking, "What's coming? How can I drastically improve what's coming and make my future months and years into genuine victories? How can I truly live my life purpose?"

And write the ideas that come to you down on this horizon page. It's really powerful. You can just write your ideas on normal lists, or you can spread them around the page for fun. You can even borrow from other brainstorming methods and write your ideas in clusters if you want.

Double Up!

Note that Horizon Brainstorming is really two brainstorms in one because you start by asking, "What's coming?" and "What's ahead for me?" and then you follow up in the second color of ink by asking, "How can I make this the future I truly want?"

You can even post a color copy of your completed horizon brainstorm on your vision board if you choose. All of this is profound because it

> Listening to audios from great leaders who are on the path of leadership, innovation, and success will help your auditory mind get on the same page as your thinking mind and visual mind.

brings your visual mind into your work—aligning it with your goals instead of leaving your thinking mind and your visual mind on separate paths.

Listening to audios from great leaders who are on the path of leadership, innovation, and success will help your auditory mind get on the same page as well. This kind of alignment can keep self-defeating thoughts and behaviors from ruining your goals and attempts at success.

Moreover, these visual notes that capture and store your brainstorming ideas (along with great audios that you listen to) help get your emotions on board with your purpose, goals, and plans as well. This is all essential to effective leadership. Top leaders do these things because they know that a person divided against him- or herself won't find much success.

Also, the visual notes in your brainstorming notebook or posted on your storyboard, horizon board, or vision board are able to immediately upgrade your "success" emotions—in a way that few things can.

> **The right visual input can snap your emotional state to where it should be in a fraction of a second.**

Where reading the right kind of books or listening to the right kind of audios can bring your emotions to the right place in minutes or hours, the right visual input can snap your emotional state to where it should be in a fraction of a second.

The Trek

Another helpful kind of brainstorm is the Trek—getting away from normal surroundings (work, home, commuting, etc.) for a couple of hours and experiencing new places, sights, sounds, and feelings. This can immediately open creativity and innovation to a higher plane.

Despite its name, the Trek doesn't have to mean three days of hiking to a peak above 15,000 feet or across a desert in boots to protect against snakes or cactus. It can be as simple as leaving the house or office for two hours and going to a park.

The change of scenery — sitting on a bench, glancing up occasionally to see bikers passing by, and hearing children laughing from the playground, the sound of birds in the trees, or a stream running past — can do wonders for your creativity and innovation centers.

Such a change of scenery tends to flip your innovational switch, so to speak. The key is changing things up. Of course, if your daily work is at the park amid such sounds and sights, you're likely to get a creative boost by putting on your suit and going to an office building or bank waiting room.

As you notice the people all dressed up for their profession, hear the sounds of meetings and intercoms and elevators, and rub the soles of your dress shoes on the marble under your seat, your "this is different" brain will click on, and your innovational neurons will perk up.

> **Variety really is the spice of life when you're trying to engage more creativity and muster a higher level of innovation.**

Variety really is the spice of life when you're trying to engage more creativity and muster a higher level of innovation. Pull out your notebook, and start brainstorming.

A Trek brainstorm can take you to a bookstore, a restaurant, or a hot tub. The trick is to go somewhere you don't go very often.

Make It Fun

This is precisely the reason that a lot of business is done on golf courses — because the change of scenery opens the mind to new, different, creative alternatives and possibilities. Just going on a drive can be very helpful, as long as you stop, park, and write your innovative ideas in your notebook. If you don't write them, you haven't brainstormed.

A variation on the Trek is a Culinary Trek, where you try a new food, something you've never tasted before. New tastes really can open your mind up to new thoughts. Just have your notebook ready to capture the ideas.

Likewise, if you have a serious challenge in your work or personal life, and you need truly great, excellent creativity and innovational thinking to take it on, do a two-day or even longer Trek. This can be a vacation to a place you've never been before, like those outlined in the book *Ladder* (part of the LIFE Leadership Essentials Series). Or it can be a seminar or convention.

To truly boost your innovative thinking to a much higher level, attend a conference or workshop on a topic unrelated to your typical work. It may be community preparedness (many towns and cities offer such training), gems (taught by a master jeweler), surfing, motocross, sword making, a Ferrari museum, Shakespeare festivals, martial arts competitions, a class on pruning trees, or a book club discussion on Tolstoy. The sky is the limit on what's offered out there.

If you look for something out of your normal wheelhouse, you'll find many options. Choose something you are at least a bit interested in but haven't pursued much in the past. Then go, take notes, and keep your brainstorming notebook handy.

You'll be amazed at how many new, innovative ideas will bombard your mind in this new setting—ideas that relate directly to your work. Surrounded by a very different subset of people than your usual experience and hearing about all kinds of new things, your creative brain will jump into overdrive.

We're not suggesting that you do this a lot, since focus is needed to master your life mission and your life goals. You don't want to just flit around from field to field, topic to topic, never gaining true mastery. That's a recipe for wasting your time and money.

But when you run into a major problem and need a huge shot of innovative help, jumping into a very different kind of gathering or study than you've ever experienced will nearly always catalyze a meteor shower of innovative creativity. Write your ideas down on paper, and you'll be excited with how many powerful solutions will come.

Follow Up

After your brainstorm, but only *after*, switch gears and spend some time analyzing what you have on paper. Some of the ideas will be perfect for your needs; others will require more thought and work, and some won't ever make it past the pages of your notebook. But all of them will help you keep thinking innovatively.

For the ideas that you decide to actually apply, use the six stages of successful innovation. Don't just let them dwindle away as ideas; turn them into realities. And as you are making some of your best ideas real, keep additional ideas coming. This is very important.

The more truly creative ideas you generate in your weekly brainstorm session—and the more creative ideas you capture in your brainstorm notebook—the more innovative ideas you'll be able to bring into reality. Without innovation, leadership dwindles; and without a consistent source of good ideas, innovation always shrinks.

> **The more truly creative ideas you generate in your weekly brainstorm session—and the more creative ideas you capture in your brainstorm notebook—the more innovative ideas you'll be able to bring into reality.**

THE MASTERMIND

Alone we can do so little.
Together we can do so much.
—Helen Keller

Brainstorm early; brainstorm often. Also, brainstorm alone, and sometimes brainstorm with a group. The Mastermind is simply the brainstorm done in a group setting, instead of alone. But when you get together with like-minded leaders to brainstorm and plan, the creative power is multiplied by the quantity and depth of brains taking part in the process.

> When you get together with like-minded leaders to brainstorm and plan, the creative power is multiplied by the quantity and depth of brains taking part in the process.

Moreover, synergy kicks in, and you end up using more brainpower than the mere sum of the minds in the room. This concept, taught by Buckminster Fuller and popularized by Earl Nightingale and Stephen Covey, among others, is a powerful tool.

Top leaders don't just brainstorm consistently, to infuse real innovation into their work and also to keep their innovative skills sharp. They also frequently brainstorm in a Mastermind group.

If you don't have such a group, wisely develop one. You don't want to fill your Mastermind group with people who emphasize lots of discord and argument, for example, because synergy will multiply their negativity. Not helpful.

Three Character Traits

The best Mastermind groups are made up of like-minded, like-hearted, and like-committed people. What does this all mean?

To be *like-minded* means that you share values, such as achievement, excellence, integrity, and mutual support. If someone doesn't share the group's values (e.g., integrity, hard work, or frugality), the Mastermind will be limited in its effectiveness.

Like-hearted consists of being willing to share, to give in to others when you realize they are right, to remain humble, to sacrifice for the whole, etc. Successful people often have strong egos, and when they are humbly like-hearted, they'll work together instead of at odds with each other.

Thus their strength of will and ego combine to create even more success than the individuals could have accomplished alone.

> **Successful people often have strong egos, and when they are humbly like-hearted, they'll work together instead of at odds with each other.**

Like-committed people share the same goals. They want to bring about the same overall objectives, both as a group and by their influence in the world. They are also committed to these goals. They really care and are willing to work hard, sacrifice, and do whatever is needed to help make the goals a reality.

Again, if members of the Mastermind team have divergent goals or even different agendas, or some members are fully committed while others are just dabbling in the project, this can weaken the Masterminding power of the group.

But being like-committed does not mean having the same temperament. Not at all. Some Mastermind members can be quiet, while others are loud. Some can be brash, while others are more accommodating. And some can be intense, while others are relaxed.

In fact, the more diversity of style and personality you have in a Mastermind team, the better. This creates a wide range of ideas and innovations—as long as all members are truly like-minded, like-hearted, and like-committed.

Allies

There is also another kind of Mastermind team member who is invaluable to effective innovation. This is the *ally*, the person who isn't part of the decision-making arm of the Mastermind team but sometimes participates in the creative and innovative elements of team success. If you don't have such allies, your Mastermind team will be weakened because you'll tend to focus on inner ideas and unwittingly but inevitably adopt a "not invented here" or "things invented here are better than other things" mentality.

Nearly all successful Mastermind teams struggle with this. They became successful based on "things invented here," by the inner workings of their team, so they are loath to look outside. In many, indeed in most, aspects of leadership, this serves them well. But when it comes to innovation and creativity, the outside voice of an ally or two will very often win out over a "closed" Mastermind.

Good allies are like-minded and like-hearted, as described above, but they don't need to be like-committed. In fact, they are better allies when they don't share the same specific organizational goals as the Mastermind team. They are great allies if they have the same level of commitment for their own areas of focus and leadership.

This allows them to bring a different view of issues to the Mastermind group—to infuse it with an outside perspective that can make a huge difference and create a lot more true innovation. Since most organizations and leadership teams face the problem of innovation-killing groupthink (where only inside views are "allowed"), the ideas of an ally can significantly open up positive thinking about new, creative, much-needed innovations.

Mastermind teams that don't have such allies can approximate great innovation by bringing in outside readings and other works and discussing how such articles, books, audios, or other materials apply to them. This can be helpful, but it still isn't as effective as periodically seeking out the non-insider views, thoughts, ideas, and suggestions of trusted allies.

In fact, in addition to the normal Mastermind meetings that a team engages to deal with issues, make plans, innovate as needed, and improve, the best leaders hold special Mastermind events once in a while where they bring in an ally or two for discussions on major needs—and brainstorm possible innovations and solutions that could make a real difference.

This kind of process is where the concept of consulting came from, but full-time consultants are usually a less effective substitute for real allies and the wisdom and innovative ideas they bring.

Three Groups

To put this all in practical terms, if you are a leader, you need:

1. A community that is working with you to build something important (your company, your business, your department, etc.)

2. A Mastermind group, a close-knit team of like-minded, like-hearted, and like-committed leaders who help you innovate, establish goals, plan, execute the plan, and achieve the goals

3. Allies who are leaders in their own sphere (separate from yours) whom you can tap periodically to give you honest, frank feedback and outside suggestions for improvement and who can sometimes join your Masterminding to help with specific innovations

Mastermind Brainstorming

While the Mastermind group will do many things, one of the most important is to purposely innovate. Again, as with all Masterminding, the goal is to generate more brainpower through the team approach than you would have through brainstorming alone.

If you are skilled at personal brainstorming and practiced at doing it consistently each week, you'll be a quality resource when your Mastermind team turns its attention to creativity and innovation.

> **With Masterminding, the goal is to generate more brainpower through the team approach than you would have through brainstorming alone.**

As a Mastermind group, try the same kind of brainstorming techniques discussed in the last chapter. But do them together as a group. For example:

- Write down ideas generated by the Mastermind team. Put them either on a board for all to see or on a large easel notebook so you can save the pages. If you use a whiteboard, have someone record the ideas on paper or electronically.

- Separate the "creative idea generation" from any analysis of ideas. Only analyze and discuss the pros and cons of ideas after you have completed the brainstorming.

- Review the ideas from last time your team met and brainstormed. Mention both the ideas that were adopted and those that weren't. Such review helps the creativity begin to flow in the room.

- Invite anyone to go to the board at any point and write down ideas. This brings an equality to the group and encourages the shy people or those who are still hatching a new idea to feel comfortable getting thoughts out in the open.

- Have someone in front writing down ideas, so that a person who doesn't want to stand up will still share.

- As appropriate, use PeopleStorming to get the group discussing specific people and how to learn from them, include them in something, or help them. Announce a strict "no gossip" or "only positive" rule to this. Nothing shuts down quality, effective brainstorming like an open gossip or criticism session. If the focus is positive, however, PeopleStorming in a Mastermind can be extremely helpful.

- Use Storyboarding as needed to get the innovative ideas flowing on large or complex questions or projects with many moving parts. The person writing the ideas on the board should be familiar with Storyboarding techniques from his or her own brainstorming.

- Storyboarding is one of the most effective brainstorming methods in a Mastermind setting. Use multiple pages as needed. If you are using the recommended large easel notebook, rip off pages and tape them on the board or (where possible) the walls so you can Storyboard many idea clusters at a time. And using sticky notes or cards that you tape or pin on the storyboard can make it easy to reorganize your ideas later.

- Don't stick to one topic! Let the innovation clusters run wild, and capture the ideas. You can (and should) analyze and discuss them all later.

- If Mastermind members disagree about ideas, write both views down in the idea clusters. In fact, write down three, four, or twenty differing ideas. You can sort them out later. For now, the more innovative views, the better.

- If you are facing some major problems, challenges, or opportunities, use your Mastermind brainstorming to come up with truly excellent responses or innovations. Use Vision Boarding, Horizon Brainstorming, or a group Trek to get out of rut thinking and spur the "group mind" to new ideas and possibilities.

  If you know you'll be brainstorming some big challenges, have a corkboard, tacks, and a diverse collection of magazines in the back of the room—just in case a vision board might spark new thinking, better ideas, and more positive feelings.

  Don't use it unless the time is right, but if it seems potentially helpful, go all in and inspire your Mastermind team to really go for it! This always encourages new creativity and innovative thinking.

  Again, if your main purpose for the brainstorm is to deal with a major challenge or opportunity or a change of direction for a better future, a Horizon Brainstorm can be very effective. Simply draw the horizon on the board, tell the Mastermind group that it's a horizon, and ask them what's coming in the months ahead and what's likely to come just over the horizon.

Ask them what their fears and dreams are, and get those out in the open and on the board for everyone to discuss. At the right time, this can be extremely positive and effective.

- Once their fears and dreams are on the board, ask, "How can we overcome the fears and ensure the dreams?" And get the ideas flowing. This can be a profound Mastermind event.

- If the focus is not on some major challenge but rather on getting better growth or increasing quality through innovative improvements, include a trusted ally or two in the event. Hire them as consultants, if needed, and really include them in the brainstorming. Their outside views will be invaluable to your team. And their thoughts on your horizon views will make a huge positive contribution to your organization and leadership.

- Use a Trek when you really want to get everyone thinking in new ways, and plan it well so there is a good balance between fun times and Mastermind meetings. Whereas a Trek can be very simple for your personal weekly brainstorm session, it is more complex when you include a full Mastermind team.

Still, sometimes it is exactly what is needed. Get together, get away, and then talk—a lot—and watch the magic happen. A well-planned Mastermind group Trek can do a great deal of the heavy lifting for you and bring out the best innovation your team has hidden away inside.

Simple Can Be Great

Remember that some of the most important and most effective innovations are simple improvements on what you already have—on the parts of your business that are working well. These typically come because of a routine weekly personal brainstorm or a routine annual or semiannual Mastermind brainstorming event.

So don't scrimp on Mastermind brainstorming. Give it time, focus, and resources. If you do it consistently and make it enjoyable, it will provide huge dividends in innovational progress for your organization. Also, make it special for those who attend so that they look forward to the next event. Excited participants have more and better ideas.

DON'T CANNIBALIZE

*In preparing for battle I have always found that plans are
useless, but planning is indispensable.*
—Dwight D. Eisenhower

E very time you innovate, you introduce changes that will have an
impact on the things you are already doing. Sometimes the consequences of your innovation are
clear beforehand, but sometimes they
aren't. When you innovate and it
brings unintended or surprising results, sometimes you have new
problems.

**Use the brainstorming
techniques outlined in
this book to forecast
and think through what
will happen when you
announce and roll out
a new innovation.**

Thus it is important for top leaders to
think about the potential consequences
of innovative changes well before they
are introduced. Use the brainstorming
techniques outlined in this book to forecast and think through what will
happen when you announce and roll out a new innovation. Figure out
as many potential changes as you can beforehand.

Why It Matters

The main purpose of this second-tier brainstorming on any
innovation is to make sure you don't compete with yourself. It's to
ensure that innovations won't reduce or steal from your current goods
and services or mess anything up unintentionally.

For example, let's say you offer service X. You have a long history of providing service X, and many people love it and repeatedly purchase it for their use. They enjoy working with your company, and they spread the popularity of your service by sharing their positive feelings with friends and other people they know.

Make sure you don't compete with yourself, and ensure that innovations won't reduce or steal from your current goods and services.

Over time, you build your business and have 10,000 clients consistently purchasing service X. Nice. You ask your customers what other services they would like, and you get a lot of positive feedback.

Three major suggestions stand out, and you brainstorm ways to roll them out and hopefully quadruple your sales. You bring in your Mastermind team and brainstorm how to innovatively offer these new services, and you apply all six stages of successful innovation.

As you put the three new products through the stages, you realize that two of them aren't going to be as effective as you had hoped. But with good focus and team interaction, you bring service Y to the point of a truly excellent innovation. Your team runs the numbers, and you all get excited about doubling your offering.

You'll continue to provide service X, as always, and now you'll also offer service Y. You assume that at least half of those getting service X will also want service Y, so you plan accordingly.

In fact, you think that over time, more than half of those consistently enjoying service X will want to add service Y to their life. "It's such a great service, after all," you tell yourself. "And the customers themselves asked for it."

You and your team do the work, get service Y ready, and offer it to the world. It's a great day, and you celebrate with your leadership team.

Then, over the next few days and weeks, a strange thing happens, something you didn't expect. Within two months, it's confirmed: half of your consistent service X customers are sticking with X and haven't purchased Y. That's what you thought would happen, so you're not shocked.

But instead of the other half of your customers adding service Y to their purchase list and keeping service X as well, they do something else. They add service Y, which is what you had hoped, but they stop buying service X. They just switch.

They still spend the same amount they always did. Thus you are left in an interesting place. You now bring in the same amount of gross income that you did before you introduced service Y. But there's a problem. You are getting the same amount of income, but you are spending a lot more because you are now producing and supporting two services instead of just one.

Big Problems

As a result, your gross income is the same as it used to be, but your net profit has gone down significantly! "That's not an innovation," you realize. "It's a disaster. We doubled our costs but didn't increase our actual income."

This is one way that some companies cannibalize themselves, and this exact process gets a lot of would-be Innovators in trouble.

The good news is that it usually only happens once to a leader before he or she learns to never do it again! The even better news is that you can learn the principles in this chapter and never do it at all.

Solutions

How do you avoid cannibalizing your own business when you innovate? The answer: specifically include the question of cannibalizing in your brainstorming and planning. Ask: "How will this innovation compete with our current offerings? How can we make sure it doesn't compete with our own products and services? In fact, how can we structure things so that the new offering *increases* sales of our current services and products?"

This is a vital part of any effective innovation. Ask these questions long before you fully develop an innovation. In fact, ask them during Stage 2 of the effective innovation system, while you are still in Creation mode. Then work the answers into both the Creation and Experimentation stages of your innovation planning.

This is extremely important. When you ask these questions early, it becomes easy to make innovations that increase your current income levels—and don't detract from them. For example, sometimes it's as easy as pricing. You might simply promote service Y as the next level of service X, and price it accordingly.

> When you ask the right questions early, it becomes easy to make innovations that increase your current income levels—and don't detract from them.

To use a specific example: Let's say that service X, which you've built up over time and which has a long history of positive customer support, costs the typical customer $200 a month. If you announce the new service Y at $200 a month, many customers will naturally see the two services as competing options. They'll consider both and choose one to purchase.

If you price service Y at $150 or $100, you'll likely see a wholesale shift in your customer base from service X to service Y. Many people will simply choose the cheaper service—if they are in any way similar.

But if you promote the new service as an add-on and price it accordingly, you'll get a lot of people who decide to buy both. For example, you could only make service Y available to those who purchase service X and price the total for both at $295. So the customer has the choice of service X for $200 or both services for $295.

Of course, your team would have to work on the price during Stages 2 and 3 (Create and Experiment) to be sure you can actually generate a profit at that price point. And you'll want to run the numbers early so you can determine whether this is, in fact, a good innovation. It might initially seem like a good idea but turn out to cost too much in the long run.

Explore More Options

Another option is to make service Y a premium service and price it at $395. This allows customers to keep service X or jump to service Y— but any who jump pay enough to justify the switch.

There are many other options, but the Innovator has to see them before doing all the effort and work of Stages 3–5 and then finding out there's a problem. Don't cannibalize your own business. Don't compete with yourself. Think through each innovation with these types of questions in mind.

Put as much brainstorming and wise thinking into the potential consequences and surprise ramifications of an innovation as you do into the product or service itself.

You want to put as much brainstorming and wise thinking into the potential consequences and surprise ramifications of an innovation as you do into the product or service itself. And your leadership team needs to think through every possible scenario you can imagine and come up with a wise approach.

Innovation Is for Champions

The Horizon Brainstorming method can be especially helpful to you and your team in this process.

When you deal with innovation this way, the surprises will be fewer and less frequent — and they'll often be positive surprises rather than negatives to your bottom line.

Of course, beyond the finances, good innovators also think through how new innovations will impact quality, usability, public relations, marketing, and other characteristics of the product, service, or company. During innovation, use a lot of creativity to consider potentialities. There is also communication and how to roll out your innovation, for instance. These matters can't be ignored.

Innovation isn't for the weak or impatient. It is the work of champions. Learn to get it right as often as possible, by brainstorming more than good ideas. Also brainstorm and Mastermind the potential consequences of each innovation, and lead accordingly.

KEEP DOING YOUR CORE

Be yourself; everyone else is already taken.
—Oscar Wilde

This tactic may seem obvious, but it's amazing how predictably many inexperienced leaders or new innovators make this mistake. Just consider:

- Your business is growing.

- You run into challenges (because growth is always challenging).

- You wish there were an easier way.

- You have an idea.

- You think of all the ways it might make things easier.

- You decide to just do it (without following all six stages of effective innovation; in fact, you may not even know about the stages when you make this decision).

- Implementing this new idea takes a lot of your time, effort, and focus—more than you expected.

- As a result, a few things slip in other parts of your life.

- As you put more energy and time into this new, "easier" approach, the very features that were making your business grow begin to slip.

- Your business stops growing.

- You keep working on this new, easier way. You just "know" that it's going to work! "I'm changing everything!" you tell yourself.

- Your business begins to shrink.

What to Do with "Easy"

The true Innovator knows that this isn't the way to do things. If you ever find yourself trying to create "the easier way," stop! Shift gears, and refocus on doing things "the effective way" and especially "the right way." Do things the way that has given you (and others) success.

> If you ever find yourself trying to create "the easier way," stop! Shift gears, and refocus on doing things "the effective way."

Then—and only then—put a bit of your energy into doing things "a better way." That's innovation. It's "90% perspiration, 10% inspiration," as the old saying goes.

The 10% is powerful because it creates a consistent emphasis on improving and creatively innovating, but the key to success is to do both the 90% and the 10%. In fact, most top leaders will tell you that they'll choose a person who is a 90% grinder and just keeps doing the hard work, over a 10% "innovator" who is always considering an easier way to do things.

But in truth, such an "innovator" isn't really an Innovator at all. He or she wants to be innovative, but unless the 90% perspiration is there, it's just not going to work.

In contrast, add 10% innovative energy to a person who is consistently performing the 90% work, day in and day out, and you've got the makings of a great leader. But the 90% simply must be there. Period.

> No work, no victory.

No work, no victory.

In Addition, Not Instead

The 90% work takes guts, grit, determination, and tenacity. And it eventually always wins, if it keeps going. Add an additional 10% creative innovation, and you've got something very special. That's what innovation is all about—the real kind, the type of innovation that actually works, the kind that applies all six stages and makes a genuine, lasting difference.

So yes, innovate! Absolutely. But don't let the things that are working slide. Keep doing them, and innovate *in addition* to them—not *instead* of them.

> Don't let the things that are working slide. Keep doing them, and innovate *in addition* to them— not *instead* of them.

This is crucially important. Again, most top leaders have learned this lesson by blowing it at least once! And they've learned that any undertaking is a lot harder when you blow it and then have to regroup and start over. You can follow that path, or you can learn from their experience.

Real wisdom comes when you learn from others and apply the lessons they've already learned and taught. This is the path to genuine excellence in leadership. You'll get your share of the lessons that come from making your own mistakes—every leader does. But wherever possible, learn from others and avoid repeating their mistakes.

The principle directly applies to this tactic: *Keep Your Core*. Don't stop doing the things that have brought success and growth. And then, in addition, include that 10% more in creative innovations. The wannabe innovator, the poser, thinks that everything should be changed and aims for a 90% or, even more frequently, a 100% overhaul.

The Innovator—genuine, effective, consistent, vibrantly creative—always wins the victory because he or she keeps doing the things that work and then adds just a little more in creative innovations to stay on the cutting edge.

DON'T INSTITUTIONALIZE

It's not hard to make decisions when you
know what your values are.
—Roy Disney

Remember how important it is to be nimble? Well, sadly, many organizations make the mistake of becoming too institutional. This makes them less agile and always reduces the level of innovational creativity in their organizational culture.

The goal is growth in quality, effectiveness, service, customers, organizational value, and profits without growth in institutionalism and its inevitable bureaucratic drag. It has been said that every organization starts out with important ideals but then faces struggles, turns its focus to survival, and grows to the point where its major focus is simply more growth.

But true leaders emphasize growth without forgetting the real goals!

Don't Lose Your Way

While there is nothing wrong with the goals of survival and growth, when an organization's primary emphasis is growth rather than the ideals that truly matter, the organization has lost its way. It may grow (many such organizations do), but it is now institutional—meaning that its real purpose is merely to expand the institution rather than add something great, meaningful, valuable, and wonderful to society.

When an organization gets caught in this trap of institutionalism ("by the institution, of the institution, for the institution"), it loses what makes it vibrant, unique, and truly important. This is a sad development for any organization. If it once stood for something really significant or great, this step into mediocrity is a tragedy.

What to Do?

How do you, as a leader, help your organization avoid institutionalism? The answer is simple, if not always easy: Keep the organizational purpose at the forefront of all leadership and executive decisions, policies, and organizational behaviors.

> **Keep the organizational purpose at the forefront of all leadership and executive decisions, policies, and organizational behaviors.**

As Peter Drucker taught, this only works if the top leaders of the company maintain this approach.[99] The CEO, president, or whoever is the top executive (e.g., director, chairman of the board, or equivalent in the organization), must keep this in mind at every turn.[100] Every speech, organization-wide communication, and event must openly and even blatantly emphasize the organization's purpose.

This isn't needless repetition, and it doesn't get old. It is a clear focus on what matters, a true vision of the organization's central purpose.

Other things can and should be covered, of course, but the purpose must never be left out or taken for granted. It can never just be assumed. It must always be explicitly mentioned and held up as the standard.

Any slip from this approach is a step toward institutionalism. As Drucker taught, this is the one thing that nobody except the CEO (or the top leader, regardless of job title) can do effectively.[101]

And while this is the express job of the top executive, it should also be exemplified by the governing board and other top leaders.[102]

The more widespread this focus on the true, great purpose of the organization, the better.

Avoid Any Institutionalism

Such focus on the main purpose can be difficult, given that the CEO and other organizational leaders are busy and have to deal with multiple tasks, issues, people, and challenges. At times, other concerns may seem or feel more pressing. But nothing is ever more pressing than the purpose; if it is, then institutionalism has kicked in.

To remain an innovative organization, avoid institutionalism, and stay on purpose. Indeed, keep the purpose in mind when making every decision, policy, and innovation.

DON'T OVER-PROFESSIONALIZE

No man ever followed his genius till it misled him.
—Henry David Thoreau

To avoid becoming institutionalized, don't professionalize. This does not mean to stop being professional. Professionalism is certainly very important to organizational success.

Instead, this tactic means something else altogether: Organizations that want to stay on purpose and effectively grow and accomplish their purpose must not overload their offices with positions, departments, and tasks that can be effectively (and more efficiently) outsourced.

This may seem obvious, but it is an essential part of being the Innovator—as a leader and as a company. In short, the more overstuffed your professional staff, the less innovative you'll tend to be.

Where possible, outsource.

> **The more overstuffed your professional staff, the less innovative you'll tend to be.**

Act Wisely

Of course, there are certain roles that simply must be done in-house to get the best results. Leaders wisely keep these close. Note that such roles differ, depending on what kind of business you are in and where you are located. (Different laws and industries demand different choices in regard to full-time professionals on staff.)

That said, without unwisely getting rid of professionals who are best maintained full-time and on site, it is important to be conscious and deliberate about this. Make a plan, and plan effectively. Have professionals on staff as needed, but don't have more than you should.

> **Have the full-time professionals that you need on hand, outsource others, and don't overstaff when outsourcing would be just as effective.**

Especially in the Information Age, many professional services are literally just a computer screen away. Slowing down innovations just a bit to gain the wisdom of proven professionals is often helpful and shouldn't be avoided. It will frequently save you headaches down the road.

But over-professionalizing your full-time organization will be detrimental to a long-term culture of innovation. Again, be wise and exact about this. Have the full-time professionals that you need on hand, outsource others, and don't overstaff when outsourcing would be just as effective.

This Increases Innovation

The truth is that many top professionals will be more innovative — and thus actually add to your organizational culture of innovation — when running their own firms or practices than they would be working in your company as corporate professionals. In their own organization, they'll necessarily rise to leadership by taking on innovative effectiveness rather than tending to hold it back.

The best innovative professionals (from law and marketing to inventors and artists) are often found leading their own companies. Success for their business demands innovative leaders and promotes them, just as it does for any other type of organization.

As a result, when they work with you to fulfill your professional needs, you get top innovators as well as top professionals. This is nearly always a plus. And the opposite — bureaucracy — is always anti-innovation.

TACTIC 7

DON'T POLITICIZE

*Politics is the art of looking for trouble, finding it
whether it exists or not, diagnosing it incorrectly, and
applying the wrong remedy.*
—Sir Ernest Benn

Another key tactic for successful leaders and innovators is to avoid politicization. In any group of people, politics can rear its ugly head. Working in an organization where the rules and leaders say one thing publicly but then leaders grant back-room deals with a few people (for whatever reason) and exclude others from these special benefits is very frustrating.

That's politics in the workplace, and it's a negative wherever it shows up. It's demoralizing, destructive, and detrimental to further success, growth, and leadership.

Avoid Institutional Anti-Innovation

In fact, such political climates create an institutionalized culture where most employees and leaders stop trusting the organization. Not only is this bad for business, but it eats away at a culture of innovation.

Why would a genuine leader or the Innovator want to work in a system that is rigged? The best leaders in such a group will naturally begin to look elsewhere.

> **When politics infects an organization, even a little bit, quality innovation dries up.**

When politics infects an organization, even a little bit, quality innovation dries up. It is replaced by people using their creativity to innovate new ways to be "on the inside," to benefit from the special deals of the favored few.

By Any Other Name...

In government, this is known as corruption. In some nations of the world, it is the normal mode of doing business and is called bribery or "greasing the skids." Note that such nations nearly always have struggling economies.

> **Politicization tends to turn innovation toward the wrong ends and hurts the overall growth of an organization.**

Politicization tends to turn innovation toward the wrong ends and hurts the overall growth of an organization. If allowed to last, this problem always creates major negatives for the organization.

Open and Equal

This doesn't mean that there can't be special benefits, perks, or incentives for performance. It just means that such rewards must be openly announced and honestly earned. Politicization enters into an organization when back-room or special rule-breaking benefits are handed out by leaders like Caesars in ancient Rome.

Such politicization didn't end well for Rome, and it always hurts companies that allow it to continue. Don't politicize! It's very bad for your organization's purpose and future. It's terrible for innovation, and it undermines leadership.

If you are a leader, root it out wherever it appears—immediately and consistently. This will win you the reputation of being fair, firm, and a person of principle. All of these qualities are essential to effective leadership.

Moreover, rooting such politics out of your organization will greatly encourage a lasting culture of innovation—not to mention integrity and trust.

BUILD AN INNOVATIVE SOCIETY!

Innovation is the specific instrument of entrepreneurship...the act that endows resources with a new capacity to create wealth.
—Peter F. Drucker

This brings us to the conclusion of our journey through the principles of effective innovation. Every leader needs it, and so does every organization.

But before we're done, let's address our central question once again: What does it take to become the Innovator? It's certainly not an easy path exempting you from work, learning important lessons, or giving your all.

Becoming the Innovator is a life focus for top leaders and anyone who wants to become a real leader. Like any worthwhile effort, it takes energy, hard work, and follow-through.

But those who do it, who keep at it until they become effective Innovators, know that it is well worth the effort. Those who can consistently

> **Becoming the Innovator is a life focus for top leaders and anyone who wants to become a real leader.**

innovate know how to turn any challenge or problem into an excellent opportunity and significant progress.

They know how to see something that is working well and improve it even more. They know how to turn a 20 percent success rate into something much better and even how to make a 100 percent success into a true 110 percent victory! That's powerful.

It's also leadership.

It is leadership of the highest order, in fact. Without effective innovation, all leaders hit a ceiling, get caught in a rut, or watch their results plateau—even when their efforts keep increasing. Innovation opens doors, brings new opportunities, and creates whole new possibilities.

Leadership!

Without innovation, there is always stagnation. In fact, as Newton's laws state, a body will continue in its current motion and trajectory unless acted upon by something else.

> **Without innovation, there is always stagnation.**

Innovation is that "something," the action that brings change, increases success, and ensures improvement. The Second Law of Thermodynamics states it simply: in a closed system, disorder increases. This means that without innovation, without initiative, without new action, things won't just improve on their own. In fact, they'll get worse—naturally.

We have to take action to make things better—in our finances, in our relationships, in our level of happiness, and, indeed, in everything. If we want our lives to be better, we must act. And we must act in the right ways, ways that work.

The people who take such action are leaders. The actions they take are innovations. It really is this simple.

Indeed, these two powerful concepts—leadership and innovation—are inseparably connected. They are partners. They work together. When quality leadership increases, effective innovations are being created. And when excellent innovations are occurring, leaders are focused and at work.

If you want to be a better leader, learn to be a more effective innovator. As you do so, you'll become the kind of leader who not only innovates but teaches others to innovate—and in turn, to teach yet others to innovate as well.[103]

> **If you want to be a better leader, learn to be a more effective innovator.**

Be a Game Changer

To be the Innovator, you'll also spread three game changers that help promote innovation in your organization and beyond—in society as a whole. Note that these game changers can only be effectively implemented by leaders.

Game Changer #1: Exemplify!

Set an example of innovative leadership by applying the six stages, the strategies, the tactics, and the other tools of innovation covered in this book. As Orrin Woodward teaches, example is the most important part of leadership. Without it, everything else a leader says or tries to teach will fall on deaf ears. Example *is* leadership.

Exemplify effective innovation, and you'll see many Innovators rise up among those you lead.

Game Changer #2: Challenge!

Once you are exemplifying innovative leadership, challenge those you lead to be innovators. Challenge them to consistently improve things, to learn the six stages of effective innovation by heart and apply them constantly, and to adopt the strategies and tactics that together create the Innovator's worldview. Call on them to become true Innovators in every important walk of life.

Challenge them to learn to think like Innovators and to teach the principles of innovation covered in this book to everyone they lead. This will naturally spread the values and skills of innovation much further than they would be without such leaders championing them.

Game Changer #3: Incentivize!

With the first two game changers in place, add a third. Create targets and incentives for those who effectively innovate. This can be as simple as sharing their stories and new techniques or improvements with the whole organization. After this happens a few times, almost everyone will want to innovate effectively.

> **Use Brainstorming and Masterminding to establish the wisest and most effective incentives for your organization and customers.**

More elaborate incentives can also help encourage real, quality innovation. In fact, if your organization already has an incentive program, make sure it gives excellent rewards to those who innovate.

Use Brainstorming and Masterminding to establish the wisest and most effective incentives for your organization and customers.

Also, be sure that incentives emphasize true innovation, not just Stage 1 ideas or the *desire* to innovate.

The Last Word

Remember that innovation can come from surprising sources. When you as a leader exemplify, challenge, and incentivize innovation and when you teach the stages and principles of effective Innovators, you'll create an environment where innovation can arise from anyone.

This creates and maintains a thriving organizational culture. And it will spur increased innovation and improved leadership throughout your business and community.

For example, the story is told of a young man on D-Day during World War II. While some of the details are unconfirmed, the overall lesson of the story is profound.[104]

As you know, the Allied forces invaded the entrenched Axis troops holding Europe by storming the beaches at Normandy. The battle was almost lost before it could get started, however, because the tanks kept getting stuck in huge pits the enemy had built up and down the beach.

In the midst of battle, the young soldier, without rank or authority, realized what was needed. As a farmer at home, he had learned how to get tractors past similar pits using logs to propel them up and over the bogs to higher ground. He saw the situation and thought this method would work with the tanks.

In many armies through human history, this lowly soldier's ideas would have remained unknown and unheeded. He would have been too scared to share the innovation with his superiors, or they would have quickly put him in his place and told him to "shut up and follow orders."

But in Eisenhower's army, a different culture was carefully maintained. Good ideas were welcomed and rewarded. So the young man shared the idea with his unit leader, and they immediately put it to work.

They didn't wait for orders. In the dire circumstances of bullets and shells flying dangerously around them, they took action. They innovated. It was effective. The tanks cleared the pits, and the balance of the battle shifted.

The unit leader passed the new information up the chain of command, and soon tanks were jumping the pits all along the beach. Just imagine a lowly private telling captains and majors what to do and how to do it! Innovation is powerful. It is a vital facet of leadership. Without it, all leadership idles or stalls.

Innovation Is Power

Effective innovation changes everything because it changes the right things — at the right time.

When this happens, progress is the inevitable result. Success always depends on the right kind of innovation at the right time. In other words, the world needs the Innovator.

The Innovator turns defeat into victory, decline into reform, and triumph into long-term improvements. The Innovator turns success into even better success and then even more success. The Innovator is a leader, and every great leader is the Innovator.

In fact, even budding leaders can be the Innovator. And if they keep at it, such Innovators always become better, more effective leaders.

Moreover, when Innovators keep focused on their great life purpose, many important things get done in the world. If there are great inventions, increased opportunities, improved standards of living, increased happiness, better businesses and communities, and healthier, wiser, better lives, somewhere behind all these successes stands a certain kind of person: the Innovator.

> **Even budding leaders can be the Innovator. And if they keep at it, such Innovators always become better, more effective leaders.**

There is a reason that many of today's leaders, writers, and business experts keep teaching that innovation is vital to our societal success. Behind every success and all advancement—there stands the Innovator.

There stands one who didn't accept that "things are just the way they are." There stands one who knew that things could be better. There stands one who faced real challenges and just kept fulfilling his or her life purpose—in the face of whatever opposition and difficulties arose.

There stands the Innovator.

If there is progress, know this: Somewhere behind it all, there stands one who helped build a team of leaders to change the world for good. There stands the Innovator.

Everywhere in the world, at any time and in every arena of struggle and endeavor, if there is *any* improvement, there is the Innovator.

If you want improvement and greater success in your life and for your family, career, business, or future, you have one choice. There is only one way. One path will get you there:

Become the Innovator.

NOTES

1   *Coastal Living*, May 2015, 62.

2   Ibid.

3   Ibid.

4   Citations from this section come from William Deresiewicz, "The Death of the Artist and the Birth of the Creative Entrepreneur," *The Atlantic*, January/February 2015.

5   Ibid., 96.

6   Stefan Thomke and Jim Manzi, "The Discipline of Business Experimentation," *Harvard Business Review,* December 2014, 71.

7   Nathan Furr and Jeffrey H. Dyer, "Leading Your Team into the Unknown," *Harvard Business Review,* December 2014, 82, 84.

8   David K. Hurst, "Greasing the Skids of Innovation," *strategy+business*, Winter 2014, 83–84. See also Alex Pentland, *Social Physics: How Good Ideas Spread – The Lessons from a New Science* (New York: The Penguin Press, 2014).

9   See the excellent article: Scott D. Anthony, David S. Duncan, and Pontus M.A. Siren, "Build an Innovation Engine in 90 Days," *Harvard Business Review*, December 2014, 60–68.

10   See ibid for more details and commentary.

11   Art Kleiner, "The Thought-Leader Interview: Zhang Ruimin," *strategy+business*, Winter 2014, 98.

12   Ibid. See also Samuel Greengard, *The Internet of Things* (Cambridge, MA: MIT Press, 2015).

13   Ibid. See also Jennings Brown, "Connectedness: A Reckoning," *Esquire,* May 2015. According to Brown, in 2015 there are approximately 15 billion "connected devices"; by 2020 there will likely be 50 billion.

14   Ibid.

15   See Oliver DeMille, *Freedom Matters* (Cary, NC: Obstaclés Press, 2015).

16   See Ram Charan, Michael Useem, Dennis Carey, "Politicians for Prosperity," *strategy+business*, Winter 2014, 6.

17   Thomke and Manzi, "The Business Experimentation," 70-79.

18   See Tom Foster, "Maker Inc.," *Popular Science*, January 2015, 56–75.

19   Details and description in Ibid., 59.

20   John Adams, *Discourses on Davila*, "Discourse IV."

21   C. S. Lewis, "The Inner Ring."

22   Ibid.

23   Barry Jaruzelski, Volker Staack, and Brad Goehle, "Proven Paths to Innovation Success," *strategy+business*, Winter 2014, 34–49.

24   Ibid., 41–45.

25   Ken Blanchard and Sheldon Bowles, *Raving Fans: A Revolutionary Approach to Customer Service* (New York: William Morrow & Company, Inc., 1993).

26   See also Brant Cooper and Patrick Vlaskovits, *The Entrepreneur's Guide to Customer Development*.

27   Jaruzelski et al., "Proven Paths to Innovation Success," 42–43, 45.

28   James Fallows, "The Tragedy of the American Military," *The Atlantic*, January/February 2015.

29   Ibid., 74.

30   Ibid., 73.

31   Ibid., 74.

32   Ibid.

33   Deresiewicz, "Death of the Artist," 94–95.

34   Ibid., 96.

35   Ibid., 92.

36   Jaruzelski et al., "Proven Paths to Innovation Success," 42–45.

37   Ibid.

38   See Geoffrey Moore, *Crossing the Chasm*.

39   Jaruzelski et al., "Proven Paths to Innovation Success," 46.

40   Ibid., 49.

41   Jane Porter, "Fast Track to the Corner Office," *Men's Health*, January/February 2015, 101.

42   Ibid., 102–104.

43   Jaruzelski et al., "Proven Paths to Innovation Success," 42.

44   Ibid.

45   *The Atlantic*, November 2014, 84, volunteer online survey.

46   Ibid.

47   Ibid., 83.

48   See Ken Kurson, "Let It Pour," *Esquire*, Jan/Feb 2015, 42.

49   Chris Brady and Orrin Woodward, *Financial Fitness: The Offense, Defense, and Playing Field of Personal Finance*, second edition (Cary, NC: Obstaclés Press, 2015), 126–128.

50   See Michael Gerber, *The E-Myth Revisited* (New York: HarperCollins Publishers, 1995).

51   These levels are discussed in detail in Robert Kiyosaki, 1998, *Rich Dad's CASHFLOW Quadrant*, 81–96.

52   More commentary on this list in Brady and Woodward, *Financial Fitness*, 145–151.

53   Ibid., 151–152.

54   Ibid., 152.

55   Ibid., 152–153.

56   Ibid., 153.

57   Bruce Grierson, "Eureka!" *Psychology Today*, March/April 2015, 1.

58   Ibid., 50.

59   Ibid.

60   Ibid., 53. (Quoting Mark Beeman, a cognitive neuroscientist at Northwestern University.)

61   Ibid., 54–56.

62   Ibid., 56–57.

63   Ibid., 57.

64   Ibid.

65   Ibid.

66   Ibid.

67   Ibid., 54.

68   Ibid.

69   Ibid.

70   Ibid.

71   Ibid.

72   Ibid.

73   Ibid.

74   Ibid.

75   Ibid., 49.

76   See Guy Winch, "Harm from a Handheld," *Psychology Today*, March/April 2015, 37–38.

77   Holly Pevzner, "Building the Perfect Day: Hack Your Routine to Make Every Hour Count," *Psychology Today*, January/February, 2015, 70–79, 77.

78   Ibid.

79   Ibid., 75.

80   Emma Seppälä, "This Is Your Brain on Gmail," *Psychology Today*, January/February 2015, 12.

81   Ibid.

82   See "Joining Together with Many Others Can Spark Personal Epiphanies," *Psychology Today*, March/April 2015, 17. See also Joshua Wolf Shank, *Powers of Two: How Relationships Drive Creativity* (New York: Houghton Mifflin Harcourt Publishing Company, 2014).

83   See, for example, Ibid., "Joining Together…"

84   Jaruzelski et al., "Proven Paths to Innovation Success."

85   Catharine P. Taylor, "Brand Diving," *strategy+business*, Winter 2014, 69–72.

86   Ibid.

87   Ibid.

88   See Oliver DeMille, *A Thomas Jefferson Education: Teaching a Generation of Leaders for the Twenty-First Century* (Cedar City, UT: George Wythe College Press, 2006).

89   Taylor, "Brand Driving," 69.

90   See Seth Godin, *Tribes: We Need You to Lead Us* (New York: Portfolio, 2008); Alvin and Heidi Toffler, *Revolutionary Wealth: How It Will Be Created and How It Will Change Our Lives* (New York: Alfred A. Knopf, 2006).

91   Olaf Acker, Germar Schröder, Florian Gröne, "Kings of the Cloud," *strategy+business*, Winter 2014, 22-27.

92   See, for example, Joe Keohane, "Economy Plus," *Esquire*, May 2015. See also John H. Richardson, "How Much Better Can We Stand To Be?," *Esquire*, May 2015. See also Tim Harford, "The Modern Price of Getting a Table," *The Atlantic*, May 2015.

93   See Ken Blanchard and Sheldon Bowles, *Raving Fans*.

94   See Robert K. Greenleaf and Larry C. Spears, *Servant Leadership*.

95   Cited in Foster, "Maker Inc.," 61.

96   Foster, "Maker Inc.," 58.

97   Stephen R. Covey, *The 7 Habits of Highly Effective People* (New York: Simon & Schuster, 2004).

98   Cited in Oliver DeMille and Ed J. Pinegar, *Parenting Made Easy*, manuscript.

99   Peter Drucker, *The Effective Executive* (New York: HarperBusiness, 2006).

100   Ibid.

101   Ibid.

102   Ibid.

103   Chris Brady and Orrin Woodward, *Launching a Leadership Revolution*, second edition (Cary, NC: Obstaclés Press, 2015).

104   Source unknown.

Other Books in the LIFE Leadership Essentials Series

Mentoring Matters: Targets, Techniques, and Tools for Becoming a Great Mentor with Foreword by Orrin Woodward
Get your sticky notes ready for all the info you're about to take in from this book. Do you know what it means to be a *great* mentor? It's a key part of successful leadership, but for most people, the necessary skills and techniques don't come naturally. Educate yourself on all of the key targets, techniques, and tools for becoming a magnificent mentor with this easy-to-apply manual. Your leadership success will be forever increased!

Turn the Page: How to Read Like a Top Leader with Introduction by Chris Brady
Leaders are readers. But there are many ways to read, and leaders read differently than most people do. They read to learn what they need to know, do, or feel, regardless of the author's intent or words. They see past the words and read with the specific intent of finding truth and applying it directly in their own lives. Learn how to read like a top leader so you'll be better able to emulate their success. Applying the skills taught in *Turn the Page* will impact your life, career, and leadership abilities in ways you can't even imagine. So turn the page and start reading!

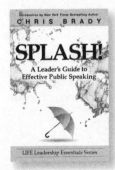

SPLASH!: A Leader's Guide to Effective Public Speaking with Foreword by Chris Brady
For many, the fear of giving a speech is worse than the fear of death. But public speaking can be truly enjoyable *and* a powerful tool for making a difference in the lives of others. Whether you are a beginner or a seasoned orator, this book will help you transform your public speaking to a whole new level of leadership influence. Learn the SPLASH formula for great public speaking that will make you the kind of speaker and leader who makes a SPLASH—leaving any audience, big or small, forever changed—every time you speak!

The Serious Power of Fun with Foreword by Chris Brady

Life got you down? Feeling like life isn't much fun is a bad place to be. Fun matters. It is serious business and a source of significant leadership power. Without it, few people maintain the levels of inspired motivation and sustained effort that bring great success. So put a smile back on your face. Discover how to make every area of life more enjoyable and turn any situation into the right kind of fun. Learn to cultivate a habit of designed gratification—where life just keeps getting better—and *laugh your way to increased success* with *The Serious Power of Fun!*

Wavemakers: How Small Acts of Courage Can Change the World with Foreword by Chris Brady

Every now and then, extraordinary individuals come along who make huge waves and bring about permanent change in the lives of so many that society as a whole is forever altered. Discover from the examples of the various "Wavemakers" showcased in this book how you can make waves of your own and change the world for the better!

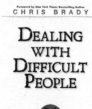

Dealing with Difficult People with Foreword by Chris Brady

How many times have you felt like banging your head against the wall trying to figure out how to deal with a routinely difficult person, whether at work or in your personal life? You can't control others, but you can control how you handle them. Learn about the seven main types of difficult people and the Five-Step Peace Process, and equip yourself to understand why people behave the way they do, break the cycle of frustration, and turn your interactions into healthy, productive experiences. "You are going to encounter difficult people. Plan on it. Prepare for it. Become good at it."

***Financial Fitness for Teens: 6 Steps from Broke to Abundant with Foreword* by Chris Brady**

It's never too early to learn the principles of financial success. But schools often skip right over this crucial topic. And by the time many adults figure out that they don't know how to properly manage their money, they are often buried in debt and feeling helpless to dig themselves out. *Financial Fitness for Teens* aims to fill in the gap, break the cycle of bad financial habits and misinformation being passed down from generation to generation, and show youth how easy and exciting financial fitness can be. "The money thing" is one of the most important aspects of life to master — and the sooner, the better!

***Conflict Resolution: The 8 Vital Principles* with Foreword by Tim Marks**

Conflict Resolution is more than just reading words in a book. It's about utilizing what you learn in order to keep moving forward without negative baggage and drama. Tend to difficult situations properly, and instead of winning battles, you will win allies. This book will completely equip you to learn how to handle situations with grace, calmness, and strength. It takes courage to resolve conflict rather than to just run from it or ignore it. Your quality of life depends on it. With the right information, properly applied, your life can be peacefully productive.

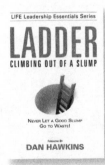

***Ladder: Climbing Out of a Slump* with Foreword by Dan Hawkins**

Stuck in a rut and feeling your dreams are out of reach? Stop listening to the negative voices telling you success is too hard and that you aren't good enough. Your slump is screaming that it's time for a change. And the Slump-to-Success Ladder is your friend that will help you turn your slump into increased success. Once you know the art of climbing the simple but powerful Six Rungs of the Slump-to-Success Ladder, you will have much more control over where you end up. So when a slump comes, you will smile and enthusiastically start climbing the Ladder right away, knowing that success is on the way!

Subscriptions and Products from
LIFE Leadership

Rascal Radio Subscription
Rascal Radio by LIFE Leadership is the world's first online personal development radio hot spot. Rascal Radio is centered on LIFE Leadership's 8 Fs: Faith, Family, Finances, Fitness, Following, Freedom, Friends, and Fun. Subscribers have unlimited access to **hundreds and hundreds** of audio recordings that they can stream endlessly from both the **LIFE Leadership website** and the **LIFE Leadership Smartphone App.** Listen to one of the preset stations or customize your own based on speaker or subject. Of course, you can easily skip tracks or "like" as many as you want. And if you are listening from the website, you can purchase any one of these incredible audios.
Let Rascal Radio provide you with **life-changing information to help you live the life you've always wanted!**

The LIFE Leadership Series
Here's where LIFE Leadership began—with the now famously followed 8 Fs: Family, Finances, Fitness, Faith, Following, Freedom, Friends, and Fun. This highly recommended series offers a strong foundation on which to build and advance in every area of your daily life. The timeless truths and effective strategies included will reignite passion and inspire you to be your very best. Transform your life for the better and watch how it will create positive change in the lives of those around you. Subscribe today and have the time of your LIFE!

Series includes 4 audios and 1 book monthly and is also available in Spanish and French.

The AGO (All Grace Outreach) Series

We are all here together to love one another and take care of each other. But sometimes in this hectic world, we lose our way and forget our true purpose. When you subscribe to the AGO Series, you'll gain the valuable support and guidance that every Christian searches for. Nurture your soul, strengthen your faith, and find answers to better understand God's plan for your life, marriage, and children.

Series includes 1 audio and 1 book monthly.

The Edge Series

You'll cut in front of the rest of the crowd when you get the *Edge*. Designed for those on the younger side of life, this hard-core, no-frills series promotes self-confidence, drive, and motivation. Get advice, timely information, and true stories of success from interesting talks and fascinating people. Block out the noise around you and learn the principles of self-improvement at an early age. It's a gift that will keep on giving from parent to child. Subscribe today and get a competitive *Edge* on tomorrow.

Series includes 1 audio monthly.

The Freedom Series Subscription (12 Months)

Freedom must be fought for if it is to be preserved. Every nation and generation needs people who are willing to take a stand for it. Are you one of those brave leaders who'll answer the call? Gain an even greater understanding of the significance and power of freedom, get better informed on issues that affect yours, and find out how you can prevent its decline. This series covers freedom matters that are important to *you*. Make your freedom and liberty a priority and subscribe today.

Subscription includes 1 audio monthly for 12 months.

LLR Corporate Education Program

Based on the *New York Times* bestselling book Launching a Leadership Revolution, the LLR Corporate Education Program is designed not just to *train employees* but to *develop leaders*.

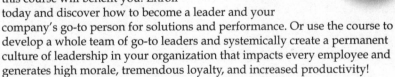

Leadership development is perhaps the single most important investment any company can make. *The leader creates the culture; the culture delivers the results.* So whether you're an employee, an HR manager, or a business owner, this course will benefit you. Enroll today and discover how to become a leader and your company's go-to person for solutions and performance. Or use the course to develop a whole team of go-to leaders and systemically create a permanent culture of leadership in your organization that impacts every employee and generates high morale, tremendous loyalty, and increased productivity!

6-month subscription course includes 1 book and 4 audios monthly. Optional tests included at no additional charge.

FINANCIAL FITNESS PROGRAM

Get Out of Debt and Stay Out of Debt!

FREE PERSONAL WEBSITE
SIGN UP AND TAKE ADVANTAGE OF THESE FREE FEATURES:

- Personal website
- Take your custom assessment test
- Build your own profile
- Share milestones and successes with partners and friends
- Post videos and photos
- Receive daily info "nuggets"

FINANCIAL FITNESS BASIC PROGRAM

The first program to teach all three aspects of personal finance: defense, offense, and playing field. Learn the simple, easy-to-apply principles that can help you shore up your resources, get out of debt, and build stability for a more secure future. It's all here, including a comprehensive book, companion workbook, and 8 audios that amplify the teachings from the books.

Also available DIGITALLY!

FINANCIAL FITNESS MASTER CLASS

Buy it once and use it forever! Designed to provide a continual follow-up to the principles learned in the Basic Program, this ongoing educational support offers over 6 hours of video and over 14 hours of audio instruction that walk you through the workbook, step by step. Perfect for individual or group study.
6 videos, 15 audios

FINANCIAL FITNESS TRACK AND SAVE

The Financial Fitness Program teaches you how to get out of debt, build additional streams of income, and properly take advantage of tax deductions. Now, with this subscription, we give you the tools to do so. The Tracker offers mobile expense tracking tools and budgeting software, while the Saver offers you thousands of coupons and discounts to help you save money every day.